STATE OF CALIFORNIA—BUSINESS, CONSUMER SERVICES AND ⌐

BUREAU OF SECURITY AND IN
P.O. Box 98
West Sacramento, C⌐
(916) 322-⌐
www.bsis.ca.gov

MW01201686

SECURITY GUARD
(FACT SHEET)

REQUIREMENTS FOR REGISTRATION

A security guard must have in his/her possession a valid security guard registration or a screen-print of the Bureau's approval from the Bureau's web site at www.bsis.ca.gov, along with a valid photo identification, before working as a security guard.

Security guards are employed by licensed private patrol operators to protect persons or property and prevent theft. To be eligible to apply for a security guard registration, you must:

- Be at least 18 years old
- Undergo a criminal history background check through the California Department of Justice (DOJ) and the Federal Bureau of Investigation (FBI); and
- Complete a 40-hour course of required training. The training and exam may be administered by any private patrol operator or by a Bureau certified firearm training facility.

40 Hour Security Guard Training Requirement

Date of Completion	Training Hours Needed
Prior to Submitting an Application or Being Assigned to a Post	8 Hours
Training Required within the First 30 Days	16 Hours
Training Required within the First Six Months	16 Hours
TOTAL HOURS	**40 HOURS**

EXPEDITE PROCESSING

In order to speed up the security guard application and fingerprinting process, the following steps should be followed:

STEP 1

The security guard must have received the eight (8) hour "Power to Arrest" training and passed the examination.

STEP 2

The security guard applicant, private patrol operator or the training facility must submit the security guard application online at http://www.bsis.ca.gov/online_services/online_licensing.shtml. The online application is sent electronically to the Bureau.

Breakdown of fees paid online:

Security Guard Application Fee	$50.00
On-Line Convenience Fee	$ 1.00
TOTAL	$51.00

STEP 3

The security guard applicant must submit fingerprints electronically using Live Scan. You must only use the Security Guard Live Scan form downloaded from the Bureau's web site or obtained from the Bureau. The Bureau's Live Scan form contains the correct coding to ensure that the Bureau receives the FBI and DOJ responses.

Breakdown of fees paid at Live Scan site:

Department of Justice Fingerprint Fee	$32.00
Federal Bureau of Investigation Fingerprint Fee	$17.00
TOTAL	$49.00

Live Scan site locations are available at http://ag.ca.gov/fingerprints/publications/contact.php

Note: Live Scan sites may charge a Live Scan submission processing fee. The Bureau does not set the fee amount.

STEP 4

Once the Bureau has received the online application and criminal history clearances, the cleared security guard will appear on the Bureau's web site. The security guard, private patrol operator, or training facility can verify the Bureau's approval by checking the Bureau's "Verify a License" at http://www2.dca.ca.gov/pls/wllpub/wllqryna$lcev2.startup?p_qte_code=G&p_qte_pgm_code=2420.

Once the security guard registration has been cleared and appears on the Bureau's web site, a screen-print from the web site may be used as an interim security guard registration. The security guard can then be placed on assignment. The actual security guard registration will be mailed to the applicant and should be received in 10 to 15 business days.

STEP 5

Security guards placed on assignment must keep the following documents with them:

1. A valid security guard registration or a screen print of the Bureau's approval obtained from the Bureau's web site.

2. A valid photo identification

NORMAL PROCESSING

The Bureau will continue to accept the following:

*   Submit your completed security guard application, a $50 registration fee and a Security Guard Live Scan form signed by the Live Scan operator, including the ATI number. A $32 DOJ fingerprint processing fee, $17 FBI fingerprint processing fee, and Live Scan site processing fee must be paid at the Live Scan site. Send your application package to the Bureau of Security and Investigative Services, P.O. Box 989002, West Sacramento, CA 95798-9002.

Applications for registration as a security guard are available from private patrol operators or training facilities certified by BSIS.

FIREARM PERMIT

You may ***not*** carry a gun on duty without a valid firearm permit or a screen print of the Bureau's approval obtained from the Bureau's web site. Also, a firearm permit issued by the Bureau ***does not*** authorize you to carry a concealed weapon. You may ***not*** carry a concealed weapon on duty without a Concealed Weapons Permit (CCW) issued by local authorities, nor carry a caliber handgun not listed on your firearm permit.

To apply for a firearm permit, you must:

- Be a U.S. citizen or have permanent legal alien status.
- Pass a course in the carrying and use of firearms. The 14-hour (8 hours classroom, 6 hours range) training course covers moral and legal aspects, firearms nomenclature, weapon handling and shooting fundamentals, emergency procedures, and range training. The course must be given by a Bureau-certified firearms training instructor at a Bureau-certified training facility. Written and range exams are administered at the end of the course. Costs of training are determined by the training facility. For a list of certified training facilities, call (916) 322-4000.
- Submit a firearm permit application, pay the $80 application fee, and submit a Security Guard Registration w/Firearm Permit Live Scan form signed by the Live Scan site operator, including ATI number. A $38 Firearm Eligibility application, $32 DOJ fingerprint processing fee, $17 FBI fingerprint processing fee, and Live Scan site processing fee *must* be paid at the Live Scan site. Send your application package to the Bureau of Security and Investigative Services, P.O. Box 989002, West Sacramento, CA 95798-9002.

You may submit *both* a guard registration application and a firearm permit application *at the same time* to the Bureau along with a **$130** fee.

Note: A firearms qualification card expires two years from the date it was issued. An applicant must requalify four times during the life of the permit: twice during the first year after the date of issuance, and twice during the second year. Requalifications must be at least four months apart.

TEAR GAS PERMIT

The law requires those who wish to carry tear gas on duty to complete a training course approved by the Department of Consumer Affairs. For a list of certified training facilities call (800) 952-5210 or visit the Bureau's license look-up at http://www.bsis.ca.gov/online_services/verify_license.shtml and search by county.

BATON PERMIT

To carry a baton on duty, you must be a registered security guard and complete an eight-hour training course from a certified instructor. For a list of certified training facilities, call (800) 952-5210 or visit the Bureau's license look-up at http://www.bsis.ca.gov/online_services/verify_license.shtml and search by county.

If you have questions about registration as a security guard, call (800) 952-5210. If you have questions about your current guard card, call (916) 322-4000.

"Protection of the public shall be the highest priority for the Bureau of Security and Investigative Services in exercising licensing, regulatory and disciplinary functions. Whenever the protection of the public is consistent with other interests sought to be promoted, the protection of the public shall be paramount."

DEPARTMENT OF CONSUMER AFFAIRS
Bureau of Security and Investigative Services

SECURITY GUARD GUIDE

A SUMMARY OF LAWS GOVERNING THE PROFESSION

JULY 2012

TABLE OF CONTENTS

The sections in the California Penal Code that refer to "Control of Deadly Weapons" have been recodified "without substantive changes" (renumbered). The new section numbers became operative January 1, 2012 and are now mainly found in Part 6 of the Penal Code, beginning at Section 16000. The Security Guard Guide contains references to California Penal Codes as they relate to security guards and weapons. Corrections have been made to Security Guard Guide to bring it into compliance with the new section numbers.

INTRODUCTION

A Summary of Laws Governing the Profession

Terrorism awareness and crime prevention have become major issues in our society. Security guards play a crucial role in safety and security. A great burden is placed on public forces to respond to crisis situations. As a result, the consumer is turning to the private security industry to help protect neighborhoods and businesses.

The Department of Consumer Affairs (DCA or Department), Bureau of Security and Investigative Services (BSIS or Bureau), has jurisdiction over the private security industry. The authority is derived from Division 3, commencing with Section 7580 thru Section 7588.5, Chapter 11.5, Private Security Services Act in the Business and Professions Code (B & P).

This brochure explains key sections of the Business and Professions Code (B & P), Penal Code (PC) and California Code of Regulations (CCR), so security guards and law enforcement officers can be fully informed of the provisions affecting private security guards.

Security guards outnumber sworn peace officers four to one in this state, so it benefits peace officers and security guards alike to learn and understand the laws governing the security industry.

NOTE: Every effort has been made to ensure the accuracy of this compilation. Should any confusion or error occur, the law will take precedence. Please refer to the relevant legal codes for clarification.

A SECURITY GUARD'S ROLE AND RESPONSIBILITIES

- A security guard's role should be to PROTECT people and/or the property of his/her employer or contracted clients.

- A security guard's responsibility BEFORE an incident/offense has occurred should be PREVENTION.

- A security guard's responsibility during or after an incident/offense should be to OBSERVE and REPORT.

- The security guard's role and responsibilities listed in the security guard guide are at the discretion of the employer. Some employers may want their security personnel to be more proactive as long as they stay within the parameters of what is lawful regarding private person (citizen's) arrest.

SECURITY GUARD POWER TO ARREST
AND
TRAINING REQUIREMENTS

A security guard must complete 40 hours of required training and an 8-hour refresher course every 12 months after completing the 40-hour course. As part of that training, a security guard must complete an 8-hour Power to Arrest/Weapons of Mass Destruction Terrorism Awareness training course prior to submitting an application. In addition, 16 hours of training is required within the first 30 days of receiving a security guard registration, or within the first 30 days from the date of hire as a security guard. An additional 16 hours of training is also required within the first six months after receiving a security guard registration, or within the first six months of employment as a security guard.

Date of Completion	Training Hours Needed
Prior to submission of an application for a security guard registration	8 hours (4 hours of Powers to Arrest/4 hours Weapons of Mass Destruction/Terrorism Awareness Training
Training Required within the first 30 Days after receipt of registration or date of hire.	16 Hours (8 hours mandatory courses/8 hours of elective courses from training syllabus)
Training Required within the First Six Months after receipt of registration or date of hire.	16 Hours (8 hours mandatory courses/8 hours of elective courses from training syllabus)
TOTAL HOURS	40 HOURS
Annual Continuing Education Required after first year of licensure	8 Hours Annually

A brief course of study in these laws and procedures is required prior to application for a "guard card." The following code sections describe the requirements in detail.

DIVISION 3, CHAPTER 11.5, PRIVATE SECURITY SERVICES
ARTICLE 4

Business and Professions Code Section 7583.6 (Excerpt)

(a) A person entering the employ of a licensee to perform the functions of a security guard or a security patrolperson shall complete a course in the exercise of the power to arrest prior to being assigned to a duty location.

(b) Except for a registrant who has completed the course of training required by Section 7583.45, a person registered pursuant to this chapter shall complete not less than 32 hours of training in security officer skills within six months from the date the registration card is issued. Sixteen of the 32 hours shall be completed within 30 days from the date the registration card is issued.

(c) A course provider shall issue a certificate to a security guard upon satisfactory completion of a required course, conducted in accordance with the department's requirements. A private patrol operator may provide training programs and courses in addition to the training required in this section. <u>A registrant who is unable to provide his or her employing licensee the certificate of satisfactory completion required by this subdivision</u> shall complete 16 hours of the training required by subdivision (b) within 30 days of the date of his employment and shall complete the 16 remaining hours <u>within six months of his or her employment date.</u> [Emphasis added]

(d) The department shall develop and approve by regulation a standard course and curriculum for the skills training required by subdivision (b) to promote and protect the safety of persons and the security of property. For this purpose, the department shall consult with consumers, labor organizations representing private security officers, private patrol operators, educators, and subject matter experts.

(e) The course of training required by subdivision (b) may be administered, tested, and certified by any licensee, or by any organization or school approved by the department. The department may approve any person or school to teach the course.

(f) (1) On and after January 1, 2005, a licensee shall annually provide each employee registered pursuant to this chapter with eight hours of specifically dedicated review or practice of security officer skills prescribed in either course required in Section 7583.6 or 7583.7.

Business and Professions Code Section 7583.7 (Excerpt)

(a) The course of training in the exercise of the power to arrest may be administered, tested, and certified by any licensee or by any organization or school approved by the department. The department may approve any person or school to teach the course in the exercise of the power to arrest. The course of training shall be approximately eight hours in length and shall cover the following topics:

(1) Responsibilities and ethics in citizen arrest.
(2) Relationship between a security guard and a peace officer in making an arrest.
(3) Limitations on security guard power to arrest.
(4) Restrictions on searches and seizures.
(5) Criminal and civil liabilities.
(A) Personal liability.
(B) Employer liability.
(6) Trespass law.
(7) Ethics and communications.
(8) Emergency response, including response to medical emergencies.
(9) Security officer safety.

(10) Any other topic deemed appropriate by the bureau.

(b) The majority of the course shall be taught by means of verbal instruction. This instruction may include the use of a video presentation.

Business and Professions Code Section 7583.8 (Excerpt)

No employee of a licensee who performs the function of a security guard or security patrolperson shall be issued a registration card until there is proper certification by the instructor that the exercise of the power to arrest course has been taught and the employee's certification that the instruction was received has been delivered to the department.

CALIFORNIA CODE OF REGULATIONS
TITLE 16, DIVISION 7
ARTICLE 6

§628. Training in Exercising the Powers to Arrest.

(a) The course of training in the powers to arrest prescribed by the Department of Consumer Affairs pursuant to Sections 7583.6(a) and 7583.7(a) of the Business and Professions Code consists of successful completion of a course approved by the bureau in exercising the powers to arrest.

(b) Uniformed employees of private patrol operators and responding alarm agents shall take and successfully complete the training course and examination in the exercise of powers to arrest. An employee must receive a score of 100% on said examination in order to successfully complete said course.

The course of training and administration of the examination may be given by a training school approved by the bureau or by the employer or such uniformed employees provided that such employer has a designated instructor and such instructor is knowledgeable in the powers to arrest as set forth in the Standard Training Manual issued by the bureau and is able to assist employees who cannot read or write.

(c) A licensee or approved training school which administers the training and examination shall retain the examination results on bureau-approved answer sheets for a period of not less than two years or until audited by the bureau, whichever occurs first. A licensee or training facility shall certify under penalty of perjury on the employee's application for registration that such person has successfully completed the training and examination contained in the Standard Training Manual issued by the bureau.

(d) No employee may be assigned to work until he or she has completed the course referred to in subsection (a).

FIREARMS

Training and background checks are required in order to become registered as and armed security guard. The following regulations discuss training requirements, distinctions between exposed and concealed firearms, and firearm-related crimes.

CALIFORNIA CODE OF REGULATIONS
TITLE 16, DIVISION 7
ARTICLE 7

§631. Requirements for Carrying or Use of Firearms or Simulated Firearms.

(a) A registered employee shall not carry, use or possess a loaded or unloaded firearm in the performance of his duty, whether or not it is serviceable or operative, unless he has in his possession a firearms qualification card issued to him by the chief. Such card must be shown to any peace officer or bureau representative upon demand.

(b) A registered employee may not carry any replica or other simulated firearm.

631.1. Allowing the Carrying or Use of a Firearm.

(a) A private patrol or alarm company operator shall not allow an employee to carry or use a loaded or unloaded firearm, whether or not it is serviceable or operative, unless such employee possesses a firearms qualification card.

(b) A private patrol or alarm company operator may not allow an employee to carry any replica or other simulated firearm.

632. Firearms Qualification Card.

(a) The bureau shall issue a firearms qualification card to an applicant where all of the following conditions exist:

(1) The applicant is a licensed private investigator, alarm company operator, private patrol operator or registered employee of such a licensee or is employed or compensated by a lawful business or public agency as a security guard or patrol person;

(2) The applicant has filed with the bureau a completed application for a firearms qualification card on a form prescribed by the bureau, dated and signed by the applicant under penalty of perjury that the information in the application is true and correct;

(3) The application is accompanied by:

(A) Payment of the firearms qualification fee prescribed by Section 640(g).

(B) Proof, satisfactory to the bureau, of successful completion of a course approved by the bureau in the carrying and use of a firearm. Including:

1. Proof of successful passage of a written examination prescribed by the bureau. Such examination shall be based on information required to be taught pursuant to Section 635; and

2. Proof of qualifying on an approved firearm range with the caliber of weapon to be used by the applicant pursuant to Section 635.

(4) The bureau has determined, after investigation, that the carrying and use of a firearm by the applicant in the course of his or her duties presents no apparent threat to the public safety.

(b) The firearms qualification card, when issued, shall be mailed to the applicant at the address which appears on the application. In the event of the loss or destruction of the card the cardholder may apply to the chief for a certified replacement for the card, stating the circumstances surrounding the loss, and pay a $10 certification fee whereupon the chief shall issue a certified replacement for such card.

(c) Firearms qualification card does not authorize the holder thereof to carry a concealed weapon as that term is defined in Penal Code Section 26150.

AUTHORITY TO CARRY AN EXPOSED FIREARM

The Business and Professions Code and the Penal Code contain several sections that security guards must obey when they carry an exposed firearm on duty.

BUSINESS AND PROFESSIONS CODE
DIVISION 3, CHAPTER 11.5, PRIVATE SECURITY SERVICES
ARTICLE 4

Business & Professions Code Section 7583.5

(a) Every licensee and any person employed and compensated by a licensee, other lawful business or public agency as a security guard or patrolperson, and who in the course of that employment or business carries a firearm, shall complete a course of training in the exercise of the powers to arrest and a course of training in the carrying and use of firearms. This subdivision shall not apply to armored vehicle guards hired prior to January 1, 1977. Armored vehicle guards hired on or after January 1, 1977, shall complete a course in the carrying and use of firearms, but shall not be required to complete a course of training in the exercise of the powers to arrest. The course of training in the carrying and use of firearms shall not be required of any employee who is not required or permitted by a licensee to carry or use firearms. The course in the carrying and use of firearms and the course of training in the exercise of the powers to arrest shall meet the standards which shall be prescribed by the Department of Consumer Affairs. The Department shall encourage restraint and caution in the use of firearms.

(b) No uniformed employee of a licensee shall carry or use any firearm unless the employee has in his or her possession a valid firearm qualification card.

Note: It is illegal for a licensee or registrant to carry a concealed weapon on duty without a permit issued by local authorities. The firearm permit issued by BSIS only allows the security guard to carry an exposed firearm while on duty.

EXEMPTIONS FROM THE PRIVATE SECURITY SERVICES ACT

Business & Professions Code Section 7582.2 (Excerpt)

This chapter [Chapter 11.5, the Private Security Services Act] does not apply to the following:

(a) A person who does not meet the requirements to be a proprietary private security officer, as defined in Section 7574.1, and is employed exclusively and regularly by any employer who does not provide contract security services for other entities or persons, in connection with the affairs of the employer only and where there exists an employer-employee relationship if that person at no time carries or uses any deadly weapon in the performance of his or her duties. For purposes of this subdivision, "deadly weapon" is defined to include any instrument or weapon of the kind commonly known as a blackjack, slungshot, billy, sandclub, sandbag, metal knuckles, any dirk, dagger, pistol, revolver, or any other firearm, any knife having a blade longer than five inches, any razor with an unguarded blade and any metal pipe or bar used or intended to be used as a club.

...

(k) A peace officer of this state or a political subdivision thereof while the peace officer is employed by a private employer to engage in off-duty employment in accordance with Section 1126 of the Government Code. However, nothing herein shall exempt a peace officer who either contracts for his or her services or the services of others as a private patrol operator or contracts for his or her services as or is employed as an armed private security officer. For the purpose of this subdivision, "armed security officer" means an individual who carries or uses a firearm in the course and scope of that contract or employment.

(l) A retired peace officer of the state or political subdivision thereof when the retired peace officer is employed by a private employer in employment approved by the chief law enforcement officer of the jurisdiction where the employment takes place, provided that the retired officer is in a uniform of a public law enforcement agency, has registered with the bureau on a form approved by the director, and has met any training requirements or their equivalent as established for security personnel under Section 7583.5. This officer may not carry an unloaded and exposed handgun unless he or she is exempted under the provisions of Article 2 (commencing with Section 26361) of Chapter 6 of Division 5 of Title 4 of Part 6 of the Penal Code, and may not carry a loaded or concealed firearm unless he or she is exempted under the provisions of Article 2 (commencing with Section 25450) of Chapter 2 of Division 5 of Title 4 of Part 6 of the Penal Code or Sections 25900 to 25910, inclusive, of the Penal Code or has met the requirements set forth in subdivision (d) of Section 26030 of the

Penal Code. However, nothing herein shall exempt the retired peace officer who contracts for his or her services or the services of others as a private patrol operator.

PEACE OFFICER EXEMPTIONS

An active duty peace officer or a level 1 or 2 reserve peace officer may apply to be an armed or unarmed security guard. However, to carry a weapon as a security guard, a peace officer must have on his/her person, while performing the duties of a security guard, either a written authorization from his/her primary employer (law enforcement entity) giving the peace officer permission to carry a weapon while performing the duties of a security guard or the peace officer must have an exposed firearm permit issued by the Bureau. If the peace office is unable to obtain the written permission from his/her primary employer (law enforcement entity) the peace officer must apply for the firearm permit.

Most law enforcement entities will not give a peace officer written permission on their department letterhead to carry a weapon, off duty, while performing the duties of a security guard. Therefore, the peace office must usually apply for the exposed firearm permit.

An active duty and level 1 & 2 reserve peace officer is also exempt from having to submit fingerprints for the security guard registration. However, a peace officer must submit fingerprints if the officer is also applying for the firearm permit. If the peace officer is only applying for the security guard registration they have the option of submitting or not submitting fingerprints. However, if they leave their primary employment with law enforcement (retired, quit, laid off, or fired) and have not submitted fingerprints they must notify the Bureau that they are no longer with law enforcement and return the security guard registration to the Bureau within 72 hours. If they wished to continuing working as a security guard they would have to reapply as a private citizen and complete the required training along with submission of fingerprints in order to obtain a security guard registration.

Most peace officers, who work off duty as armed or unarmed security guards, prefer to submit finger prints for both the security guard and the firearm permit. This allows a peace officer to retain the security guard registration and exposed firearm permit after the peace officer retires or changes employment status, and is no longer a sworn peace officer.

APPLICABLE PENAL CODE SECTIONS
(FROM THE 2012 COMPACT EDITION)

I.   **Penal Code Section 25850 [Carrying of loaded firearms; misdemeanor]**

§25850. (a) A person is guilty of carrying a loaded firearm when the person carries a loaded firearm on the person or in a vehicle while in any public place or on any public street in an incorporated city or in any public place or on any public street in a prohibited area of unincorporated territory.

(b) In order to determine whether or not a firearm is loaded for the purpose of enforcing this section, peace officers are authorized to examine any firearm carried by anyone on the person or in a vehicle while in any public place or on any public street in an incorporated city or prohibited area of an unincorporated territory. Refusal to allow a peace officer to inspect a firearm pursuant to this section constitutes probable cause for arrest for violation of this section.

(c) Carrying a loaded firearm in violation of this section is punishable, as follows:

(1) Where the person previously has been convicted of any felony, or of any crime made punishable by a provision listed in Section 16580, as a felony.

(2) Where the firearm is stolen and the person knew or had reasonable cause to believe that it was stolen, as a felony.

(3) Where the person is an active participant in a criminal street gang, as defined in subdivision (a) of Section 186.22, under the Street Terrorism Enforcement and Prevention Act (Chapter 11 (commencing with Section 186.20) of Title 7 of Part 1), as a felony.

(4) Where the person is not in lawful possession of the firearm, or is within a class of persons prohibited from possessing or acquiring a firearm pursuant to Chapter 2 commencing with Section 29800) or Chapter 3 (commencing with Section 29900) of Division 9 of this title, or Section 8100 or 8103 of the Welfare and Institutions Code, as a felony.

(5) Where the person has been convicted of a crime against a person or property, or of a narcotics or dangerous drug violation, by imprisonment pursuant to subdivision (h) of Section 1170, or by imprisonment in a county jail not to exceed one year, by a fine not to exceed one thousand dollars ($1,000), or by both that imprisonment and fine.

(6) Where the person is not listed with the Department of Justice pursuant to Section 11106 as the registered owner of the handgun, by imprisonment pursuant to subdivision (h) of Section 1170, or by imprisonment in a county jail not to exceed one year, or by a fine not to exceed one thousand dollars ($1,000), or both that fine and imprisonment.

(7) In all cases other than those specified in paragraphs (1) to (6), inclusive, as a misdemeanor, punishable by imprisonment in a county jail not to exceed one year, by a fine not to exceed one thousand dollars ($1,000), or by both that imprisonment and fine.

(d) (1) Every person convicted under this section who has previously been convicted of an offense enumerated in Section 23515, or of any crime made punishable under a provision listed in Section 16580, shall serve a term of at least three months in a county jail, or, if granted probation or if the execution or imposition of sentence is suspended, it shall be a condition thereof that the person be imprisoned for a period of at least three months.

(2) The court shall apply the three-month minimum sentence except in unusual cases where the interests of justice would best be served by granting probation or suspending the imposition or execution of sentence without the minimum imprisonment required in this section or by granting probation or suspending the imposition or execution of sentence with conditions other than those set forth in this section, in which case, the court shall specify on the record and shall enter on the minutes the circumstances indicating that the interests of justice would best be served by that disposition.

(e) A violation of this section that is punished by imprisonment in a county jail not exceeding one year shall not constitute a conviction of a crime punishable by imprisonment for a term exceeding one year for the purposes of determining federal firearms eligibility under Section 922(g)(1) of Title 18 of the United States Code.

(f) Nothing in this section, or in Article 3 (commencing with Section 25900) or Article 4 (commencing with Section 26000), shall preclude prosecution under Chapter 2 (commencing with Section 29800) or Chapter 3 (commencing with Section 29900) of Division 9 of this title, Section 8100 or 8103 of the Welfare and Institutions Code, or any other law with a greater penalty than this section.

(g) Notwithstanding paragraphs (2) and (3) of subdivision (a) of Section 836, a peace officer may make an arrest without a warrant:

(1) When the person arrested has violated this section, although not in the officer's presence.

(2) Whenever the officer has reasonable cause to believe that the person to be arrested has violated this section, whether or not this section has, in fact, been violated.

(h) A peace officer may arrest a person for a violation of paragraph (6) of subdivision (c), if the peace officer has probable cause to believe that the person is carrying a handgun in violation of this section and that person is not listed with the Department of Justice pursuant to paragraph (1) of subdivision (c) of Section 11106 as the registered owner of that handgun.

Note: *Merely completing a course in firearms training does not authorize a security guard to carry a firearm on duty. A security guard MUST obtain a firearm permit in order to carry a firearm while on duty. A security guard who carries a firearm on duty without a valid permit could be arrested and convicted for violation of Section 25850 of the Penal Code.*

II. Penal Code Section 25400 [Carrying a weapon concealed within a vehicle or on person]

§25400. (a) A person is guilty of carrying a concealed firearm when the person does any of the following:

(1) Carries concealed within any vehicle that is under the person's control or direction any pistol, revolver, or other firearm capable of being concealed upon the person.

(2) Carries concealed upon the person any pistol, revolver, or other firearm capable of being concealed upon the person.

(3) Causes to be carried concealed within any vehicle in which the person is an occupant any pistol, revolver, or other firearm capable of being concealed upon the person.

(b) A firearm carried openly in a belt holster is not concealed within the meaning of this section.

(c) Carrying a concealed firearm in violation of this section is punishable as follows:

(1) If the person previously has been convicted of any felony, or of any crime made punishable by a provision listed in Section 16580, as a felony.

(2) If the firearm is stolen and the person knew or had reasonable cause to believe that it was stolen, as a felony.

(3) If the person is an active participant in a criminal street gang, as defined in subdivision (a) of Section 186.22, under the Street Terrorism Enforcement and Prevention Act (Chapter 11, commencing with Section 186.20) of Title 7 of Part 1), as a felony.

(4) If the person is not in lawful possession of the firearm or the person is within a class of persons prohibited from possessing or acquiring a firearm pursuant to Chapter 2 commencing with Section 29800) or Chapter 3 (commencing with Section 29900) of Division 9 of this title, or Section 8100 or 8103 of the Welfare and Institutions Code, as a felony.

(5) If the person has been convicted of a crime against a person or property, or of a narcotics or dangerous drug violation, by imprisonment pursuant to subdivision (h) of Section 1170, or by imprisonment in a county jail not to exceed one year, by a fine not to exceed one thousand dollars ($1,000), or by both that imprisonment and fine.

(6) If both of the following conditions are met, by imprisonment pursuant to subdivision (h) of Section 1170, or by imprisonment in a county jail not to exceed one year, by a fine not to exceed one thousand dollars ($1,000), or by both that fine and imprisonment:

(A) The pistol, revolver, or other firearm capable of being concealed upon the person is loaded, or both it and the unexpended ammunition capable of being discharged from it are in the immediate possession of the person or readily accessible to that person.

(B) The person is not listed with the Department of Justice pursuant to paragraph (1) of subdivision (c) of Section 11106 as the registered owner of that pistol, revolver, or other firearm capable of being concealed upon the person

(7) In all cases other than those specified in paragraphs (1) to (6), inclusive, by imprisonment in a county jail not to exceed one year, by a fine not to exceed one thousand dollars ($1,000), or by both that imprisonment and fine.

(d) (1) Every person convicted under this section who previously has been convicted of a misdemeanor offense enumerated in Section 23515 shall be punished by imprisonment in a county jail for at least three months and not exceeding six months, or, if granted probation, or if the execution or imposition of sentence is suspended, it shall be a condition thereof that the person be imprisoned in a county jail for at least three months.

(2) Every person convicted under this section who has previously been convicted of any felony, or of any crime made punishable by a provision listed in Section 16580, if probation is granted, or if the execution or imposition of sentence is suspended, it shall be a condition thereof that the person be imprisoned in a county jail for not less than three months.

(e) The court shall apply the three-month minimum sentence as specified in subdivision (d), except in unusual cases where the interests of justice would best be served by granting probation or suspending the imposition or execution of sentence without the minimum imprisonment required in subdivision (d) or by granting probation or suspending the imposition or execution of sentence with conditions other than those set forth in subdivision (d), in which case, the court shall specify on the record and shall enter on the minutes the circumstances indicating that the interests of justice would best be served by that disposition.

(f) A peace officer may arrest a person for a violation of paragraph (6) of subdivision (c) if the peace officer has probable cause to believe that the person is not listed with the Department of Justice pursuant to paragraph (1) of subdivision (c) of Section 11106 as the registered owner of the pistol, revolver, or other firearm capable of being concealed upon the person, and one or more of the conditions in subparagraph (A) of paragraph (6) of subdivision (c) is met.

BATONS

Business & Professions Code Section 7585.9 (Excerpt)

(a) The course of training in the carrying and usage of the baton, the satisfactory completion of which shall be required of applicants who wish to obtain a baton permit, shall be in the format prescribed by the Department of Consumer Affairs as delineated in the bureau's "Baton Training Manual." The course of training contained in the manual shall include, but not be limited to, the following subjects:

(1) Moral and legal aspects of baton usage.
(2) Use of force.
(3) Baton familiarization and uses.
(4) First aid for baton injuries.

(5) Fundamentals of baton handling.
(A) Stances and grips.
(B) Target areas.
(C) Defensive techniques.
(D) Control techniques.
(E) Arrest and control techniques.
(6) Examination of the subject matter as taught in the classroom and as provided by the bureau.

***

Business & Professions Code Section 7585.14 (Excerpt)

(a) A baton training facility shall issue a bureau-developed baton permit to any person who successfully completes a baton training course as described in Section 7585.9 and possesses a valid security guard registration card issued pursuant to Article 4 (commencing with Section 7583) or who has made application for that registration card. The baton permit is valid only when the holder possesses a valid guard registration card.

Business & Professions Code Section 7583.34

A licensee shall not permit any employee to carry a baton prior to ascertaining that the employee is proficient in the use of the weapon. Evidence of proficiency shall include a certificate from a baton training facility approved by the bureau which certifies that the employee is proficient in the use of the baton.

2012 PENAL CODE SECTIONS

Penal Code Section 22295 [Exemptions: Law Enforcement Officers; Uniformed Security Guards.]

§22295. (a) Nothing in any provision listed in Section 16580 prohibits any police officer, special police officer, peace officer, or law enforcement officer from carrying any wooden club or baton.

(b) Nothing in any provision listed in Section 16580 prohibits a uniformed security guard, regularly employed and compensated by a person engaged in any lawful business, while actually employed and engaged in protecting and preserving property or life within the scope of employment, from carrying any wooden club or baton if the uniformed security guard has satisfactorily completed a course of instruction certified by the Department of Consumer Affairs in the carrying and use of the club or baton. The training institution certified by the Department of Consumer Affairs to present this course, whether public or private, is authorized to charge a fee covering the cost of the training.

(c) The Department of Consumer Affairs, in cooperation with the Commission on Peace Officer Standards and Training, shall develop standards for a course in the carrying and use of a club or baton.

(d) Any uniformed security guard who successfully completes a course of instruction under this section is entitled to receive a permit to carry and use a club or baton within the scope of employment, issued by the Department of Consumer Affairs. The department may authorize a certified training institution to issue permits to carry and use a club or baton. A fee in the amount provided by law shall be charged by the Department of Consumer Affairs to offset the costs incurred by the department in course certification, quality control activities associated with the course, and issuance of the permit.

(e) Any person who has received a permit or certificate that indicates satisfactory completion of a club or baton training course approved by the Commission on Peace Officer Standards and Training prior to January 1, 1983, shall not be required to obtain a club or baton permit or complete a course certified by the Department of Consumer Affairs.

(f) Any person employed as a county sheriff's or police security officer, as defined in Section 831.4, shall not be required to obtain a club or baton permit or to complete a course certified by the Department of Consumer Affairs in the carrying and use of a club or baton, provided that the person completes a course approved by the Commission on Peace Officer Standards and Training in the carrying and use of the club or baton, within 90 days of employment.

(g) Nothing in any provision listed in Section 16580 prohibits an animal control officer, as described in Section 830.9, or an illegal dumping enforcement officer, as described in Section 830.7, from carrying any wooden club or baton if the animal control officer or illegal

dumping enforcement officer has satisfactorily completed the course of instruction certified by the Commission on Peace Officer Standards and Training in the carrying and use of the club or baton. The training institution certified by the Commission on Peace Officer Standards and Training to present this course, whether public or private, is authorized to charge a fee covering the cost of the training.

[NOTE: BSIS issues generic baton permits to be used with all categories of batons. Therefore, while a security guard is authorized to carry any type of baton while on duty, **BSIS strongly recommends that the security guard receives specific training for each type of baton the guard carries**.]

TEAR GAS

Tear gas and other chemical agents commonly used in the security professions may only be used after the proper training and certificate have been attained. The following excerpts from the Business and Professions Code explain the requirements.

DIVISION 3, CHAPTER 11.5, PRIVATE SECURITY SERVICES
ARTICLE 4

Business & Professions Code Section 7583.35

Every licensee, qualified manager, or a registered uniformed security guard, who in the course of his or her employment carries tear gas or any other nonlethal chemical agent, shall complete the required course pursuant to Section 22835 of the Penal Code.

Business & Professions Code Section 7583.36

A licensee shall not permit any employee to carry tear gas or any other nonlethal chemical agent prior to ascertaining that the employee is proficient in the use of tear gas or other nonlethal chemical agent. Evidence of proficiency shall include a certificate from a training facility approved by the Department of Consumer Affairs, Bureau of Security and Investigative Services that the person is proficient in the use of tear gas or any other nonlethal chemical agent.

Business & Professions Code Section 7583.37 (Excerpt)

The director may assess fines as enumerated in Article 7 (commencing with Section 7587). Assessment of administrative fines shall be independent of any other action by the bureau or any local, state, or federal governmental agency that may result from a violation of this article. In addition to other prohibited acts under this chapter, no licensee, qualified manager, or registered security guard shall, during the course and scope of licensed activity, do any of the following:

***

(d) Carry or use tear gas or any other nonlethal chemical agent in the performance of his or her duties unless he or she has in his or her possession proof of completion of a course in the carrying and use of tear gas or any other nonlethal chemical agent.

APPLICABLE PENAL CODE SECTIONS

Section 22835

§22835. Notwithstanding any other provision of law, a person holding a license as a private investigator pursuant to Chapter 11.3 (commencing with Section 7512) of Division 3 of the Business and Professions Code, or as a private patrol operator pursuant to Chapter 11.5 (commencing with Section 7580) of Division 3 of the Business and Professions Code, or a uniformed patrolperson employee of a private patrol operator, may purchase, possess, or transport any tear gas weapon, if it is used solely for defensive purposes in the course of the activity for which the license was issued and if the person has satisfactorily completed a course of instruction approved by the Department of Consumer Affairs in the use of tear gas.

UNIFORMS, PATCHES, BADGES, AND VEHICLES

Security guards use distinctive uniforms, security patrol cars, and other items to distinguish their status and company affiliation. To maintain the distinction between civilians, security guards, and members of the law enforcement community, these identifying items must comply with the following regulations.

BUSINESS AND PROFESSIONS CODE
DIVISION 3, CHAPTER 11.5, PRIVATE SECURITY SERVICES
ARTICLE 3

Business and Professions Code Section 7582.26 (Excerpt)

. . .

(d) No licensee, or officer, director, partner, manager, or employee of a licensee, shall use a title, or wear a uniform, or use an insignia, or use an identification card, or make any statement with the intent to give an impression that he or she is connected in any way with the federal government, a state government, or any political subdivision of a state government.

. . .

(f) No private patrol licensee or officer, director, partner, manager, or employee of a private patrol licensee shall <u>use or wear a badge, except while engaged in guard or patrol work and while wearing a distinctive uniform.</u> A private patrol licensee or officer, director, partner, manager, or employee of a private patrol <u>licensee wearing a distinctive uniform shall wear a patch on each shoulder of his or her uniform that reads "private security" and that includes the name of the private patrol company by which the person is employed or for which the person is a representative and a badge or cloth patch on the upper left breast of the uniform.</u> All patches and badges worn on a distinctive uniform shall be of a standard design approved by the director and shall be clearly visible. The director may assess a fine of two hundred fifty dollars ($250) per violation of this subdivision. [Emphasis added]. . .

(i) No private patrol operator licensee or officer, director, partner, or manager of a private patrol operator licensee, or person required to be registered as a security guard pursuant to this chapter shall use or wear a baton or exposed firearm as authorized by this chapter unless he or she is wearing a uniform which complies with the requirements of Section 7582.27.

Business and Professions Code Section 7582.27 (Excerpt)

(a) Any person referred to in subdivision (i) of Section 7582.26 who uses or wears a baton or exposed firearm as authorized pursuant to this chapter shall wear a patch on each arm that reads "private security" and that includes the name of the company by which the person is employed or for which the person is a representative. The patch shall be clearly visible at all times. The patches of a private patrol operator licensee, or his or her employees or representatives shall be of a standard design approved by the director. . .

Business and Professions Code Section 7582.28 (Excerpt)

(a) Any badge or cap insignia worn by a person who is a licensee, officer, director, partner, manager, or employee of a licensee shall be of a design approved by the director, and shall bear on its face a distinctive word indicating the name of the licensee and an employee number by which the person may be identified by the licensee.

The provisions of this section shall not be construed to authorize persons to wear badges who are prohibited by Section 7582.26 from wearing badges. . .

DIVISION 3, CHAPTER 11.5, PRIVATE SECURITY SERVICES
ARTICLE 4

Business and Professions Code Section 7583.38

A city, county, or city and county may regulate the uniforms and insignias worn by uniformed employees of a private patrol operator and vehicles used by a private patrol operator to make the uniforms and vehicles clearly distinguishable from the uniforms worn by, and the vehicles used by, local regular law enforcement officers.

QUESTIONS?

The Bureau of Security and Investigative Services is located at:

2420 Del Paso Road, Suite 270
Sacramento, California 95834

Business hours are 8:00 a.m. to 5:00 p.m. Monday through Friday; phone (916) 322-4000.

Additional copies may be downloaded from the web site at www.bsis.ca.gov or may be requested by writing to the Bureau at the above address.

DEPARTMENT OF CONSUMER AFFAIRS
Bureau of Security and Investigative Services

POWER TO ARREST TRAINING MANUAL
October 2011

STATE OF CALIFORNIA

POWER TO ARREST TRAINING MANUAL

TABLE OF CONTENTS

POWER TO ARREST TRAINING MANUAL

TABLE OF CONTENTS

INSTRUCTOR - EMPLOYER INTRODUCTION AND TRAINING REQUIREMENTS

(Listed below are sections in the California Business and Professions Code that pertain to the Powers to Arrest Manual)

Private Patrol Operator and Security Guards:

Business and Professions Code Section 7582.1(a) defines a private patrol operator and Section 7582.1(e) defines a security guard, as follows:

§7582.1(a) A private patrol operator, or operator of a private patrol service, within the meaning of this chapter is a person, other than an armored contract carrier, who, for any consideration whatsoever: Agrees to furnish, or furnishes, a watchman, guard, patrolperson, or other person to protect persons or property or to prevent the theft, unlawful taking, loss, embezzlement, misappropriation, or concealment of any goods, wares, merchandise, money, bonds, stocks,notes, documents, papers, or property of any kind; or performs the service of a watchman, guard, patrolperson, or other person, for any of these purposes.

§7582.1(e) A security guard or security officer, within the meaning of this chapter, is an **employee of a private patrol operator, or an employee of a lawful business** or public agency who is not exempted pursuant to Section 7582.2, who performs the functions as described in subdivision (a) on or about the premises owned or controlled by the customer of the private patrol operator or by the guard's employer or in the company of persons being protected.

Proprietary Private Security Officer:

Business and Professions Code Section 7574.01(e) defines a proprietary private security employer and Section 7574.01(f) defines a proprietary private security officer, as follows:

§7574.01(e) "Proprietary private security employer" means a person who has one or more employees who provide security services for the employer and only for the employer. A person who employs proprietary private security officers pursuant to this chapter at more than one location shall be considered a single employer.

§7574.01 (f) "Proprietary private security officer" means an unarmed individual who is employed exclusively by any one employer whose primary duty is to provide security services for his or her employer, whose services are not contracted to any other entity or person, and who is not exempt pursuant to Section 7582.2, and who meets both of the following criteria:

(1) Is required to wear a distinctive uniform clearly identifying the individual as a security officer.
(2) Is likely to interact with the public while performing his or her duties.

TRAINING REQUIREMENTS

Security Guard with Firearm (G with FQ) Training

§7583.5.(a) Every licensee and any person employed and compensated by a licensee, other lawful business or public agency as a security guard or patrolperson, and who in the course of that employment or business carries a firearm, shall complete a course of training in the exercise of the powers to arrest and a course of training in the carrying and use of firearms. This subdivision shall not apply to armored vehicle guards hired prior to January 1, 1977. Armored vehicle guards hired on or after January 1, 1977, shall complete a course of training in the carrying and use of firearms, but shall not be required to complete a course of training in the exercise of the powers to arrest. The course of training in the carrying and use of firearms shall not be required of any employee who is not required or permitted by a licensee to carry or use firearms. The course in the carrying and use of firearms and the course of training in the exercise of the powers to arrest shall meet the standards which shall be prescribed by the Department of Consumer Affairs. The department shall encourage restraint and caution in the use of firearms.
(b) No uniformed employee of a licensee shall carry or use any firearm unless the employee has in his or her possession a valid firearm qualification card.

Security Guard (G) Training

§7583.6. (a) A person entering the employ of a licensee to perform the functions of a security guard or a security patrolperson shall complete a course in the exercise of the power to arrest prior to being assigned to a duty location.
(b) Except for a registrant who has completed the course of training required by Section 7583.45, a person registered pursuant to this chapter shall complete not less than 32 hours of training in security officer skills within six months from the date the registration card is issued. Sixteen of the 32 hours shall be completed within 30 days from the date the registration card is issued.
(c) A course provider shall issue a certificate to a security guard upon satisfactory completion of a required course, conducted in accordance with the department's

requirements. A private patrol operator may provide training programs and courses in addition to the training required in this section. A registrant who is unable to provide his or her employing licensee the certificate of satisfactory completion required by this subdivision shall complete 16 hours of the training required by subdivision (b) within 30 days of the date of his employment and shall complete the 16 remaining hours within six months of his or her employment date.

(d) The department shall develop and approve by regulation a standard course and curriculum for the skills training required by subdivision (b) to promote and protect the safety of persons and the security of property. For this purpose, the department shall consult with consumers, labor organizations representing private security officers, private patrol operators, educators, and subject matter experts.

(e) The course of training required by subdivision (b) may be administered, tested, and certified by any licensee, or by any organization or school approved by the department. The department may approve any person or school to teach the course.

(f) (1) On and after January 1, 2005, a licensee shall annually provide each employee registered pursuant to this chapter with eight hours of specifically dedicated review or practice of security.officer skills prescribed in either course required in Section 7583.6 or 7583.7.

(2) A licensee shall maintain at the principal place of business or branch office a record verifying completion of the review or practice training for a period of not less than two years. The records shall be available for inspection by the bureau upon request.

(g) This section does not apply to a peace officer as defined in Chapter 4.5 (commencing with Section 830) of Title 3 of Part 2 of the Penal Code who has successfully completed a course of study in the exercise of the power to arrest approved by the Commission on Peace Officer Standards and Training. This section does not apply to armored vehicle guards.

(h) This section shall become operative on July 1, 2004.

§7583.7. (a) The course of training in the exercise of the power to arrest may be administered, tested, and certified by any licensee or by any organization or school approved by the department. The department may approve any person or school to teach the course in the exercise of the power to arrest. The course of training shall be approximately eight hours in length and shall cover the following topics:

(1) Responsibilities and ethics in citizen arrest.

(2) Relationship between a security guard and a peace officer in making an arrest.

(3) Limitations on security guard power to arrest.

(4) Restrictions on searches and seizures.

(5) Criminal and civil liabilities.

(A) Personal liability.

(B) Employer liability.

(6) Trespass law.

(7) Ethics and communications.

(Revised1 10/11)

(8) Emergency situation response, including response to medical emergencies.

(9) Security officer safety.

(10) Any other topic deemed appropriate by the bureau.

(b) The majority of the course shall be taught by means of verbal instruction. This instruction may include the use of a video presentation.

(c) The department shall make available a guidebook as a standard for teaching the course in the exercise of the power to arrest. The department shall encourage additional training and may provide a training guide recommending additional courses to be taken by security personnel.

(d) Private patrol operators shall provide a copy of the guidebook described in subdivision (c) to each person that they currently employ as a security guard and to each individual that they intend to hire as a security guard. The private patrol operator shall provide the guidebook to each person he or she intends to hire as a security guard a reasonable time prior to the time the person begins the course in the exercise of the power to arrest.

(e) The bureau may inspect, supervise, or view the administration of the test at any time and without any prior notification. Any impropriety in the administration of the course or the test shall constitute grounds for disciplinary action.

(f) This section shall become operative on July 1, 2004.

Proprietary Private Security Officer (PPSO) Training

7574.18. (a) Except for a person who has completed the course of training required by Section 7583.45, a person registered and hired as a proprietary private security officer shall complete training in security officer skills within six months from the date upon which registration is issued, or within six months of his or her employment with a proprietary private security employer.

(b) (1) Except as provided in paragraph (2), a course provider shall issue a certificate to a proprietary private security officer upon satisfactory completion of a required course, conducted in accordance with the department's requirements.

(2) If a proprietary private security employer administers a course of training pursuant to this section, that proprietary private security employer shall issue a certificate to a proprietary private
security officer for the completion of training in security officer skills that each proprietary private security officer is required to complete, as determined by the department, such as, but not limited to, power-to-arrest training. However, the employer shall not be required to provide a certificate for training courses provided pursuant to a curriculum adopted by the department that are specific to that employer's business and where the subject of training is not
specifically required by the department.

(c) An employer of a proprietary private security officer may provide training programs and courses in addition to the training required in this section.

(d) The department shall develop and establish by regulation a standard course and curriculum, which shall include a minimum number of hours of instruction, for the skills training required by subdivision (a) to promote and protect the safety of persons and the security of property. For this purpose, the regulations adopted by the department pursuant to Section 7574.5, as added by Chapter 721 of the Statutes of 2007, are continued in existence, and shall be amended by the department as necessary.

(e) The course of training required by subdivision (a) may be administered, tested, and certified by any proprietary private security employer, organization, or school approved by the department. The department may approve any proprietary private security employer, organization, or school to teach the course.

(f) (1) A proprietary private security employer shall annually provide each employee registered pursuant to this chapter with specifically dedicated review or practice of security officer skills prescribed in the training required in this section. The bureau shall adopt and approve by regulation the minimum number of hours required for annual review.

(2) A proprietary private security employer shall maintain at the principal place of business or branch office a record verifying completion of the review or practice training for a period of not less than two years. The records shall be available for inspection by the department upon request.

(g) This section does not apply to a peace officer, as defined in Chapter 4.5 (commencing with Section 830) of Title 3 of Part 2 of the Penal Code, who has successfully completed a course of study in the exercise of the power to arrest approved by the Commission on Peace Officer Standards and Training. This section does not apply to armored vehicle guards.

Private Investigator (PI) Training

§7542. Every licensee and qualified manager who in the course of his or her employment or business carries a deadly weapon shall complete a course of training in the exercise of the powers to arrest as specified in Section 7583.7 and a course of training in the carrying and use of firearms as specified in Article 4 (commencing with Section 7583) of Chapter 11.5. No licensee or qualified manager shall carry or use a firearm unless he or she has met the requirements of Sections 7583.23, 7583.28, and 7583.29 and has in his or her possession a valid firearms qualification card as provided in Section 7583.30. A licensee or qualified manager who possesses a valid firearms qualification card shall comply with and be subject to the provisions of Sections 7583.31, 7583.32, and 7583.37.

Alarm Company Responder (ACE) Training

§7598.1. Every person entering the employ of a licensee, performing the function of an alarm agent who responds to alarm systems shall complete a course in the exercise of the powers to arrest, prior to being assigned to a duty location responding to an alarm system. Evidence of completion shall consist of certification by the licensee or instructor that the exercise of the powers to arrest course has been taught, the date the course was taught, and certification by the employee that the instruction was received. Evidence of completion of the powers to arrest shall be maintained in the licensee's employee records and made available to the bureau upon request.
A qualified manager is not required to register under this article.

§7598.2. The course of training in the exercise of the power to arrest may be administered, tested, and certified by any licensee. The department may approve any person or school to teach the course in the exercise of the power to arrest. The course of training shall be approximately two hours in length and cover the following topics:
   (a) Responsibilities and ethics in citizen arrest.
   (b) Relationship with the public police in arrest.
   (c) Limitations on security guard power to arrest.
   (d) Restrictions on searches and seizures.
   (e) Criminal and civil liabilities.
   (1) Personal liability.
   (2) Employer liability.
The department shall make available a guide book as a standard for teaching the course in the exercise of the power to arrest. The department shall encourage additional training and may provide a training guide recommending additional courses.

§7598.3. No employee of a licensee performing the function of an alarm agent who responds to alarm systems shall be issued a firearms qualification card until proper certification by the instructor that the exercise of the power to arrest course has been taught and the employee's certification that the instruction was received has been delivered to the department.

Training Syllabus

To view the training syllabus for security guards (California Code of Regulations Title 16, Div. 7, §643) and proprietary private security officers (California Code of Regulations Title 16, Div. 7, §645), please visit the Bureau of Security and Investigative Services website (www.bsis.ca.gov).

EXAM INFORMATION

An applicant must receive a score of 100 percent on the examination in order to successfully complete the course [Title 16, California Code of Regulations (CCR) Section 628]. Trainees who fail the final examination the first time may restudy their weak areas and try again. If the trainee has difficulty understanding the material as presented in the booklet, the instructor will be expected to offer guidance. This does not mean that you are to provide the answer key along with the booklet, but rather to assist the applicant to understand the questions.

If you are an employer administering the examination, keep in mind that you may be held responsible for your employee's conduct while on duty; therefore, it is in your interest to ensure that they are properly trained. If you are a Bureau-approved instructor, you may be held liable for the conduct of those to whom you have provided instruction; therefore, it is in your interest to train the students properly.

These booklets are intended for reuse. Please be sure to caution applicants to refrain from writing in the booklets. You are responsible for making any additional copies.

STEPS TO ADMINISTERING POWER TO ARREST

Allow each person as much time as needed to finish the examination. Before beginning the examination, determine whether anyone would benefit from having the examination questions read aloud.

1.   Explain the reason for *"Power to Arrest"* and that the final score of 100 percent is required before you can sign the security guard registration application. Explain that this is an open-book examination, and that answers may be corrected before being submitted for grading. The course is intended to be a learning experience as well as a guide to understanding.

2.   Supply each applicant with a pencil and scratch paper as well as a *Power to Arrest* answer sheet. A quiet place should be provided for the examination.

3.   *Have trainees read through to Question #65.* They should read the study material and answer the questions by writing on the scratch paper provided. You may answer any questions that may arise. If you are an employer, you may wish to inform the applicants of your own company policies at this point. Discuss answers.

4.   Review the most important points in the text:

   ➤ A security guard/proprietary private security officer is *NOT* a peace officer.

   ➤ A security guard/proprietary private security officer's primary responsibility should be to protect the property or persons he or she is assigned to protect.

   ➤ The main role of a security guard/proprietary private security officer should be *PREVENTION.*

   ➤ If prevention is not possible, the role of a security guard/proprietary private security officer should be to *OBSERVE and REPORT.*

   ➤ In reporting activity, a *FACT* is an event that actually occurs. A *CONCLUSION* is a belief one reaches as a result of the existence of certain facts.

   ➤ A security guard/proprietary private security officer is an agent of the property owner and can question people on the owner's property.

   ➤ A security guard/private security officer may prevent someone from entering private property by standing in his way.

➤ A security guard/proprietary private security officer should not touch an employee's belongings when inspecting them.

➤ A security guard/proprietary private security officer's power to arrest is the same as any other private person's.

➤ *CRIMINAL LIABILITY* refers to criminal penalties that can be imposed for a wrongful act. For example, carrying a loaded weapon concealed in your jacket is a violation of the Penal Code; the criminal penalty for the offense is a fine or jail sentence or both.

➤ *CIVIL LIABILITY* refers to penalties arising from lawsuits that private persons bring against each other.

➤ A security guard's registration card does not allow the security guard to carry a weapon; the security guard must also have a valid exposed firearm permit and/or a baton certificate. It is *ILLEGAL* to carry a firearm without a firearm permit and a valid security guard registration. It is *ILLEGAL* to carry a baton without a baton permit and a valid security guard registration.

➤ A proprietary private security officer's registration card does not allow the proprietary private security officer to carry a weapon.

➤ A firearm permit and/or a baton permit **cannot** be issued a PPSO registrant.

➤ Negligence and law violations by a security guard/proprietary private security officer may cause the employer and the client to be held *CIVILLY* responsible.

➤ A security guard/proprietary private security officer *IS NOT OBLIGATED* by law to make an arrest. When he/she does make an arrest, it is called an arrest by a private person or citizen's arrest (Penal Code §837).

➤ A misdemeanor is generally a crime for which the offender can be fined and/or sentenced to county jail for a period not to exceed one year. In order for a security guard/proprietary private security officer to make a proper misdemeanor arrest, it is necessary that the security guard/private security officer actually sees or witnesses the misdemeanor offense committed or attempted in his presence.

➤ A felony is generally a crime for which the offender can be sentenced to <u>state prison for a period exceeding one year or in the case of a capital offense, executed.</u> In order for a security guard/proprietary private security officer to make a proper felony arrest, a felony must have been committed, and the security guard/proprietary private security officer must have *REASONABLE CAUSE* to believe the person being arrested committed the offense.

➤ An arrested person is called a *SUSPECT* until the court finds him/her innocent or guilty.

➤ A security guard/proprietary private security officer making a citizen's arrest must tell the suspect of the *INTENTION* to arrest, the *CAUSE* for the arrest, and the security guard/proprietary private security officer's *AUTHORITY* to make a citizen's arrest. (Penal Code §841)

➤ *REASONABLE FORCE* in an arrest situation is a degree of force reasonably needed to detain an individual and to protect oneself. (People v. Garcia, (1969) 78 Cal.Rptr. 775)

➤ If a suspect does not feel free to walk away because of a security guard/proprietary private security officer's statements and actions, he may claim to have been under arrest.

➤ A security guard/proprietary private security officer should never touch a suspect except when they are protecting a citizen, protecting their employers property, in self defense, or when necessary to use reasonable force in effecting an arrest.

➤ Upon arrest, A security guard/proprietary private security officer may search for *WEAPONS ONLY* and may search only when they have cause to believe that the arrested person is armed. This decision is at the discretion of the security guard/proprietary private security officer's employer.

➤ A suspect *MAY NOT* be legally searched for weapons until he is actually arrested. (Penal Code §846) This decision is at the discretion of the security guard/proprietary private security officer's employer.

➤ If contraband or stolen items are discovered while searching for weapons, those items should be left on the suspect, unless there is a likelihood the suspect will dispose of them. When the suspect is turned over to the peace officer, he should be notified of the discovered items. The decision regarding this statement would be at the direction of the employer. The employer may prohibit certain items from entering their business or function.

> If a private citizen has made a lawful arrest, the peace officer by law *MAY* take custody of the suspect.

> The person/security guard/proprietary private security officer who makes an arrest will be recorded as the arresting party.

5.   Administer the final exam. Have trainees write their answers on the *"Power to Arrest"* answer sheet. If they fail the first time, have them review the material again and correct the answers they missed.

6.   Have each security guard/proprietary private security officer fill out an application for registration for employment as a security guard/proprietary private security officer or alarm agent. Sign on the *"instructor's signature"* line.

THE RESPONSIBILITIES OF THE SECURITY GUARD/PROPRIETARY PRIVATE SECURITY OFFICER AND EMPLOYER

As a registered security guard/proprietary private security officer, you have certain responsibilities to the Bureau of Security and Investigative Services and your employer. In order to prevent possible denial or revocation of your registration card, it is important that you are aware of the following:

1. Security guard/proprietary private security officers must meet several requirements before they begin work. These requirements include submitting your application by mail or online (only guards can apply online at this time) with the required fees to the Bureau.

2. Submitting your fingerprints to the Department of Justice via Live Scan immediately and include a copy of the completed live scan form with the application and fees to the Bureau.

3. Livescan fingerprint are sometimes rejected by the Department of Justice and/or the Federal Bureau of Investigation (FBI) for being illegible. If the fingerprints are rejected, you will receive a reject letter from the Bureau and you will be instructed to have your fingerprints redone.

4. While on duty you are required to possess a valid security guard/proprietary private security officer registration or a screen-printout of the Bureau's approval from the Bureau's Web site at www.bsis.ca.gov, along with a valid California photo identification.

5. A proprietary private security officer may not carry a firearm or a baton.

6. A security guard, private patrol operator, private investigator or alarm agent responder who carries a gun or a baton must have a valid exposed firearm permit and/or a valid baton certificate.

7. If you move or change your address, you must notify the Bureau within 30 days, or you may be issued an administrative fine.

8. If your employer or any instructor encourages you to violate any of the above requirements, you may report him/her to the Bureau in writing.

AT THE END OF EACH SECTION OF THIS MANUAL, you will be asked several questions to assist you in reviewing how well you UNDERSTOOD and REMEMBER what you read. You will need:

- An ANSWER SHEET for the final examination,
- PAPER for answering the review questions, and
- A PEN or PENCIL.

Please get this ready. Then go on to the next page for your first review.

POWER TO ARREST TRAINING MANUAL

PART A.

THE ROLE AND RESPONSIBILITIES OF THE SECURITY GUARD/PROPRIETARY PRIVATE SECURITY OFFICER AND EMPLOYER

It is important to remember:

> As a security guard/proprietary private security officer, you are *NOT* a peace officer!!!

How are security guard/proprietary private security officers *DIFFERENT* from peace officers?

> Security guard/proprietary private security officers *do not* have:
>
> ➢ The same job duties as peace officers;
> ➢ The same training; or
> ➢ The same powers as peace officers, according to the law.

What happens when a security guard/proprietary private security officer *PRETENDS* to be a peace officer?

> Any security guard/proprietary private security officer who *pretends* or even implies (lets others think) that he is a peace officer is *committing a crime*. A person who is found guilty of impersonating a peace officer could be punished by a *fine* and or *county jail* sentence and his registration may be denied or revoked.

What are a security guard/proprietary private security officer's *ROLES AND RESPONSIBILITIES*?

> A security guard/proprietary private security officer's role should be to *PROTECT* people and property for his employer.
>
> A security guard/proprietary private security officer's responsibility *BEFORE* an incident/offense has occurred should be *PREVENTION*.
>
> A security guard/proprietary private security officer's responsibility *DURING* or *AFTER* an incident/offense has occurred should be to *OBSERVE* and *REPORT*.

How should security guard/proprietary private security officers PERFORM their job?

The major responsibility of a security guard/proprietary private security officer ~~is~~ should be prevention *BEFORE* an incident/offense occurs. Thus, a security guard/proprietary private security officer should be *highly visible*. By being seen, the security guard/proprietary private security officer may discourage anyone who might be considering theft, damage, or personal injury. A security guard/proprietary private security officer's job focus should be *PREVENTION*. To do the job well, the security guard/proprietary private security officer *MUST*:

➢ **Be alert**
➢ **Listen**
➢ **Watch**

The decision on how the security guard/proprietary private security officer should react to any given situation is at the discretion of the security guard/proprietary private security officer's employer.

What is a sign that a security guard/proprietary private security officer is doing a good job?

The absence of incidents or offenses (crimes) is one sign that a security guard/proprietary private security officer is doing a good job.

What should a security guard/proprietary private security officer do if an incident or offense occurs?

If an incident/offense occurs, a security guard/proprietary private security officer should not immediately intervene. Instead, the security guard/proprietary private security officer should:

➢ **Stay *calm***
➢ **Observe and *remember* events**
➢ **Report to the police/or the security guard/proprietary private security officer's supervisor (follow the employer policy).**

The above direction is a suggestion and is at the discretion of the employer. Some employers may want their security personnel to be more proactive as long as they stay within the parameters of what is lawful regarding private persons (citizen's) arrest.

EXAM REVIEW NO. 1

NOW, on another sheet of paper, answer the following questions:

Q.1 THE *PRIMARY ROLE* OF A SECURITY GUARD/PROPRIETARY PRIVATE SECURITY OFFICER SHOULD BE TO:

A. Enforce the law.
B. Protect people and property.
C. Act like a peace officer.
D. Arrest law breakers.

Q.2 A SECURITY GUARD/PROPRIETARY PRIVATE SECURITY OFFICER'S ROLE IS THE SAME AS THAT OF A PEACE OFFICER.

A. True
B. False

Q.3 WHAT SHOULD THE RESPONSIBILITY OF A SECURITY GUARD/PROPRIETARY PRIVATE SECURITY OFFICER BE *BEFORE* AN INCIDENT/OFFENSE HAS OCCURRED?

A. Detain and punish.
B. Stay out of sight.
C. Prevent.
D. Search and seize.

Q.4 IT IS *AGAINST THE LAW* FOR A SECURITY GUARD/PROPRIETARY PRIVATE SECURITY OFFICER TO:

A. Arrest someone.
B. Protect property.
C. Observe and report.
D. Make someone think he is a peace officer.

1. AREAS OF RESPONSIBILITY

WHAT IS A SECURITY GUARD/PROPRIETARY PRIVATE SECURITY OFFICER'S JOB?

A security guard/proprietary private security officer is assigned to protect specific people and property. This may include detecting some of the same offenses that would cause a peace officer to act, such as a fight or burglary. But it would not include other offenses such as motor vehicle traffic violations or prostitution. This decision is at the discretion of the security guard's, PPSO's, PI's or ACE's employer.

For example, if you were on duty at a plant gate and you observed two teenagers having an auto race down a public road, you would not try to arrest them. You may decide to report it to the police if a telephone is nearby. But you were hired to protect the plant -not to arrest speeders.

(In fact, you should be *suspicious* of any activity that may draw you away from your post. It could be a *plan* to draw your attention away from your duties.)

WHAT IS A PEACE OFFICER'S JOB?

Peace officers are law enforcement officers such as Sheriffs and their Deputies, Constables, Marshals, members of city police forces and other officers whose duty is to enforce the law and preserve the public peace. If a law is violated, peace officers are required to pursue and apprehend the person responsible. This is not required of a security guard/proprietary private security officer/private investigator/alarm agent responder!

REMEMBER, a peace officer's responsibilities are different from a security guard/proprietary private security officer's responsibilities.

➢ *SECURITY GUARD/PROPRIETARY PRIVATE SECURITY OFFICERS* only protect *specific people* and *property* as directed by their employers.

➢ *POLICE (PEACE OFFICERS)* protect all people and all property and enforce laws.

WHAT OTHER DUTIES COULD A SECURITY GUARD/PROPRIETARY PRIVATE SECURITY OFFICER HAVE?

A security guard/proprietary private security officer may be responsible for maintaining certain *company rule*s established by his/her employer. These could include:

> ➢ Requiring employees to show their *badges* when entering the property;
> ➢ Inspecting *lunch pails* as employees leave the plant; or
> ➢ Monitoring *safety standards* and reporting hazards, blocked exits, fire safety, slippery floors, etc.

A security guard/proprietary private security officer's supervisor or employer most likely offer instructions on helping employees observe company rules and policies.

EXAM REVIEW NO. 2

NOW, on another sheet of paper, answer the following questions:

Q.5   YOU ARE STANDING SECURITY GUARD/PROPRIETARY PRIVATE SECURITY OFFICER INSIDE A DEPARTMENT STORE AND YOU OBSERVE TWO MEN COMING OUT OF A BAR ACROSS THE STREET. THEY START TO FIGHT. YOU SHOULD:

A. Go over and try to break up the fight.
B. Call the police if you can remain at your post.

Q.6   YOU ARE HIRED BY A BAR/RESTAURANT AS A SECURITY GUARD/PROPRIETARY PRIVATE SECURITY OFFICER. AN ANGRY CUSTOMER REFUSES TO PAY HIS CHECK. YOUR JOB IS TO:

A. Arrest him/her and everyone in his party.
B. Keep the peace and follow restaurant policy.

COMMENT: Notice the difference between situations in Questions 5 and 6. In Question 5, the fight does not relate to your responsibility at the department store. In Question 6, the customer is on your employer's premises. This dispute relates to your responsibility to protect your employer's property because a fight could damage or destroy property.

2. PREVENTION IS THE KEY

The security guard/proprietary private security officer's primary role should be to protect persons and prevent damage or destruction to property. **PREVENTION** is the key word.

For example, if you spotted some people trying to climb a fence to enter private property, you should shout at them or turn on the lights. Do anything lawful that would *discourage* their trespassing, don't wait until they cross the fence so you can arrest them.

Another typical situation might be, a person intends to steal from a store, but suddenly sees a uniformed security guard/proprietary private security officer on patrol. The person leaves the store without stealing anything. The security guard/proprietary private security officer, simply by being in uniform, has *prevented* a crime.

3. OBSERVE AND REPORT

If you can't prevent an incident, the proper action should be to *observe and report*. You should:

> ➤ *Observe carefully* and
> ➤ *Report immediately* to the local law enforcement and/or your supervisor.

SECURITY GUARD/PROPRIETARY PRIVATE SECURITY OFFICER'S ROLE

INCIDENT	SECURITY ROLE
BEFORE the incident:	*PREVENTION*
DURING OR AFTER the incident:	*OBSERVE AND REPORT and Notify law enforcement*

The above direction is a suggestion and is at the discretion of the employer. Some employers may want their security personnel to be more proactive as long as they stay within the parameters of what is lawful regarding private persons (citizen's) arrest.

4. GET HELP

If a serious offense, such as *robbery, burglary, or assault with a deadly weapon*, has been committed, *you will need* help to apprehend the suspect.

CALL THE POLICE IMMEDIATELY. Even police who are trained to make forcible arrests are encouraged to call for help in dangerous situations.

Examples:

#1:   You are patrolling the grounds of a factory at 2:00 a.m. and see two armed adults entering the stock room. What should you do? *(You should call the police, then observe and report.)*

#2:   While you are guarding a sporting goods store, a man runs out of the store. Ten seconds later, the owner runs to you and says there has been a robbery. What should you do? *(Have the owner call the police, then observe and report.)*

#3:   You are patrolling a store parking lot. A shopper loads Christmas gifts into a station wagon parked in the lot and goes back to do more shopping. The windows of the wagon are open, and three boys are gathered around the station wagon looking in. What should you do? *(You should try to prevent a possible theft by making your presence known.)*

#4:   You are on security guard/proprietary private security officer in a jewelry store. An employee showing diamond rings to a customer is called to the telephone. The customer is left alone with the display box of diamond rings. What should you do? *(You should try to discourage a theft by making your presence known.)*

The above direction is a suggestion and is at the discretion of the employer. Some employers may want their security personnel to be more proactive as long as they stay within the parameters of what is lawful regarding private persons (citizen's) arrest.

(Revised1 10/11)

PART B.

RELATIONS WITH LOCAL PEACE OFFICERS OR LAW ENFORCEMENT

Your job is made easier if you have *a good working relationship* with the local peace officers.

➢ *NEVER play "cop."* You don't have the training for it and you don't have the *legal* authority to do the same things a peace officer can do. Also, playing "cop" may antagonize the local law enforcement and hurt your company's working relations with them. Impersonating a peace officer is a felony.

➢ *DON'T MISLEAD PEOPLE.* Because of your uniform, badge, hat or other gear, some people may think you are a peace officer. *DON'T* do anything to encourage this false idea. Whenever the opportunity arises, make it a point to let them know that you are *NOT* a peace officer, but a security guard/proprietary private security officer.

➢ *DURING AN EMERGENCY,* you may not interfere with peace officers who may be on the scene even if they are on the private property of your employer or client. You must cooperate to the extent possible with these peace officers or you may be subject to arrest. Penal Code section 150 addresses aid to a peace officer, the person must be at least 18 years of age and be physically fit. If a peace officer's life is endangered citizens must render aid to the peace officer (Posse Comitatus).

REMEMBER:
Your roles are different! A peace officer is charged with the enforcement of laws in a city or county. *A security guard/proprietary private security officer is responsible for protecting only the specific people or property he is hired to protect.*

The above direction is a suggestion and is at the discretion of the employer. Some employers may want their security personnel to be more proactive as long as they stay within the parameters of what is lawful regarding private persons (citizen's) arrest.

* Note: *Posse Comitatus, literally means "power of the country".*

EXAM REVIEW NO.3

NOW, on another sheet of paper, answer the following questions:

Q.7 A SECURITY GUARD/PROPRIETARY PRIVATE SECURITY OFFICER'S LAWFUL AUTHORITY IS THE SAME AS THAT OF A PEACE OFFICER.

A. Yes
B. No

Q.8 DURING AN EMERGENCY ON THE EMPLOYER'S PROPERTY, A PEACE OFFICER INSTRUCTS A SECURITY GUARD/PROPRIETARY PRIVATE SECURITY OFFICER TO STAND OUT OF THE WAY BEHIND A POLICE LINE, THE SECURITY GUARD/PROPRIETARY PRIVATE SECURITY OFFICER MUST:

A. Refuse, as the security guard/proprietary private security officer's duties are different from those of the peace officer.

B. Cooperate and follow the lawful orders of the peace officer.

C. Apprehend the persons violating the law on the employer's or client's property since the security guard/proprietary private security officer's duty is to protect the property and person of the employer or client.

PART C

OBSERVATION AND REPORT WRITING

STOP! LOOK! LISTEN! In a sense, *security guard/proprietary private security officers are paid observers.* As a security guard/proprietary private security officer your role should be *PREVENTION.* When an offense has been committed, your responsibility should be to *OBSERVE* and *REPORT.* You may be required to:

> ➢ Report to the police
> ➢ Write a report for your employer
> ➢ Testify as to what you saw, heard, and did

The above direction is a suggestion and at the discretion of the employer. Some employers may want their security personnel to be more proactive as long as they stay within the parameters of what is lawful regarding private persons (citizen's) arrest.

FACT vs. *CONCLUSION.* You will need to know the difference between a fact and conclusion.

> ➢ A *FACT* is what has actually happened, or is known to be true.
> ➢ A *CONCLUSION* is a judgement or opinion formed as a result of the facts.

Peace officers and your employer are interested only in the FACTS. With proper facts, they can reach their own conclusions. For example:

FACT: As I came around the corner, I saw two men kneeling at the door. One was holding a crowbar. The door had markings around the lock.

CONCLUSION: The men are burglars.

Facts	Conclusion
➢ A man was walking inside of a fenced area, looking at the loading dock.	➢ A man was wandering around looking for something to steal
➢ A young man was weaving back and forth and almost fell down twice in the two minutes I observed him.	➢ He was drunk and couldn't even walk right.
➢ A Woman got into the car and tried to start it.	➢ She tried to steal the car.
➢ A girl picked up the necklace, examined it, placed in her purse, and walked directly to the north exit.	➢ After she stole the necklace, she tried to get away by the north exit.

PRACTICE MAKES PERFECT! It will take practice to become a good *OBSERVER* and to be able to *REPORT* facts instead of conclusions.

When you write a report, remember to include these six facts:

1. Who

2. What

3. Where

4. When

5. How

6. Names of witnesses

EXAM REVIEW NO. 4

NOW, on another sheet of paper, answer the following questions:

Q.9   IN ORDER TO MAINTAIN A GOOD WORKING RELATIONSHIP WITH THE LOCAL LAW ENFORCEMENT, YOU SHOULD:

    A. Never play "cop."
    B. Cooperate with local law enforcement.
    C. Both A and B.

Q. 10   WRITE AN "F" IF IT IS A FACT OR A "C" IF IT IS A CONCLUSION.

    A. He intended to kill her.
    B. She was trying to steal the ring from the jewelry counter.
    C. He ran to the fence.
    D. He opened the window and entered.

Q. 11   WHAT SIX POINTS SHOULD BE INCLUDED IN A REPORT?

DO NOT WRITE IN THIS BOOK - USE ANOTHER PIECE OF PAPER.

PART D

AUTHORITY TO QUESTION AND BASIS FOR MAKING DECISIONS

A SECURITY GUARD/PROPRIETARY PRIVATE SECURITY OFFICER'S AUTHORITY TO QUESTION PEOPLE

A security guard/proprietary private security officer is an agent of the owner of the private property and, in this role, can exercise the owner's right to ask people on the (owner's) property what they are doing there, who they are, etc. If they refuse to answer the questions or if their answers are not satisfactory, the security guard/proprietary private security officer may ask them to leave. If they do not leave, the security guard/proprietary private security officer may arrest (citizen's arrest) them for *trespassing*, and should call local law enforcement without unreasonable delay.

When on property and *not* employed as a security guard/proprietary private security officer, your authority is no greater than any other person's. On the other hand, your authority to question people is greater on property where you are *on duty as a security guard/proprietary private security officer*.

WHAT ARE THE PROPERTY OWNER'S RIGHTS?

The owner of the property has the right to establish certain rules on his property that may not be a part of the Penal Code. For instance, if an employee shows up for work drunk, he may be violating a company rule. The client may want the employee sent home or may intend to fire the employee. How this situation is handled is between the employer and the employee, and has nothing to do with the police or public law. *A SECURITY GUARD/PROPRIETARY PRIVATE SECURITY OFFICER MUST KNOW WHAT THE EMPLOYER'S POLICY STATES.*

Trying to enforce company policy could, however, result in a violation of public law, by you or by the employee.

For example, if the employee is asked to leave and refuses, he may be arrested for violating the public law against trespassing. On the other hand, if the security guard/proprietary private security officer uses unnecessary force in removing the employee from the premises, the security guard/proprietary private security officer may be arrested for committing assault and/or battery.

HOW SHOULD YOU HANDLE VIOLATIONS?

As a security guard/proprietary private security officer, acting as a representative of the owner on the owner's private property, you can physically prevent a person from entering an *area - but only as a last resort!* Be sure to check with your employer regarding the way to handle a violation of *company rules*, as well as how to handle violation' of certain *laws*.

EXAM REVIEW NO. 5

NOW, on another sheet of paper, answer the following questions:

Q. 12 ON PRIVATE PROPERTY OWNED BY YOUR EMPLOYER, YOUR AUTHORITY TO QUESTION IS:

A. No more than any private person's.
B. The same as the owner of the property and greater than that of other private parties.
C. The same as peace officer's.

Q. 13 EMPLOYEES ARE TOLD THEY MAY NOT ENTER THE FACTORY WITHOUT THEIR IDENTIFICATION BADGES. ONE EMPLOYEE SHOWS UP WITHOUT HIS BADGE AND TRIES TO ENTER. HE IS VIOLATING:

A. A company rule.
B. A public law.
C. Both a company rule and a public law.

Q. 14 IF YOU ASKED THE EMPLOYEE REFERRED TO IN QUESTION #13 TO LEAVE AND HE REFUSES, HE IS VIOLATING A PUBLIC LAW.

A. Yes
B. No

A BASIS FOR MAKING DECISIONS:

The very nature of security work requires security personnel to be constantly aware of their surroundings, the law, and the mission of private security in today's society.

Three factors to consider when making timely and reasonable decisions are:

FACTS:

> ➢ Consider the *FACTS* involved in the incident. The facts of any incident will be learned by answering the following questions:
>
> *WHO? WHAT? WHEN? WHERE? HOW? and possibly WHY?*

LAW:

> ➢ Consider the *LAWS* that may apply to the incident. Has a city, county, state, or federal *law* been violated?

POLICY:

> ➢ Consider any *POLICY* that may apply to the incident. What is the *POLICY* of your employer regarding this incident?

PART E.

INSPECTIONS

WHAT IS AN INSPECTION?

As a security guard/proprietary private security officer, your employer may enlist your assistance in conducting inspections of employees. This is not a search. Always make sure the employer has notified the employees first. Such inspections are often conducted at the end of the work day by looking into employees' cars, lunch pails, purses, or tote bags to make sure unauthorized items are not being take off the premises.

WHAT IS AN INSPECTION?

An inspection is always conducted *with the employees' cooperation*.

For example, when you want to look inside a lunch pail, purse, or tote bag, ask the employee to open it up for you to look inside. If you can't see the contents because something is in the way, ask the employee to remove the obstruction. If the employee tries to hand the item to you, politely refuse. *NEVER TOUCH THE EMPLOYEE OR HANDLE THE EMPLOYEE'S PROPERTY.*

WHAT IS AN INSPECTION?

Understand company policy. Generally, if an employee does not cooperate, you should record:

➢ Date, time, and location
➢ Name
➢ Physical description
➢ Badge ID number
➢ License number of any vehicles involved
➢ *Then* make a full report, *in writing to* your employer

The above direction is a suggestion and is at the discretion of the employer. Some employers may want their security personnel to be more proactive as long as they stay within the parameters of what is lawful regarding private persons (citizen's) arrest.

EXAM REVIEW NO. 6

NOW, on another sheet of paper, answer the following questions:

Q. 15 YOUR EMPLOYER ASKS YOU TO INSPECT THE PERSONAL BELONGINGS OF EMPLOYEES LEAVING THE PLANT. HE HAS ANNOUNCED THIS POLICY TO ALL EMPLOYEES. WHAT IS IMPORTANT TO REMEMBER ABOUT INSPECTIONS?

A. Never inspect without cooperation from the employee.
B. Never touch the employee.
C. Never touch the employee's belongings.
D. All the rules above.

Q. 16 AN EMPLOYEE WHO IS LEAVING WORK WALKS UP TO YOU AND HANDS YOU HIS LUNCH PAIL FOR INSPECTION. WHAT SHOULD YOU DO?

A. Accept it and open it to look inside.
B. Decline to take it and instead ask the employee to open it so you can inspect the contents.
C. Take it but have the employee open it.

Q. 17 YOU ARE WALKING THROUGH THE PARKING LOT AND OBSERVE COMPANY EQUIPMENT IN THE BACK SEAT OF A CAR THROUGH A CLOSED BUT UNOBSTRUCTED WINDOW OF THE VEHICLE. YOU MAY:

A. Look closely through the window (without entering the vehicle) at the equipment, and make notes which identify the equipment, the make and model of the vehicle and its license number as well as the vehicle's location in the parking lot, and render this report to your employer or client.
B. Enter the vehicle to determine if the equipment is stolen and if so take it to your employer or client.

PART F.

THE SECURITY GUARD/PROPRIETARY PRIVATE SECURITY OFFICER'S LEGAL RESPONSIBILITIES AND LIABILITIES

Actions based on poor judgement can lead to legal problems for both you and your employer. You must, by law, *avoid certain actions*. Legal responsibilities and liabilities that affect you are presented in this section.

CRIMINAL LIABILITIES

WHO HAS THE POWER TO ARREST?

The authority to arrest is given to *all private persons*. A security guard/proprietary private security officer has the same power to arrest as any other private person. However, because the security officer wears a uniform and badge, this can lead to misunderstanding and abuse.

WHAT IS AN ARREST?

An arrest is a form of lawful control by one person over the actions or movements of another. An arrest is taking a person into custody *IN A CASE* and *IN THE MANNER* authorized by law. An arrest may be made by a peace officer or a private person (citizen's arrest).

WHAT IS CRIMINAL LIABILITY?

Crimes are generally defined in penal statutes of a state, or the ordinances of local cities or counties. All persons are expected to obey these laws. Anyone who violates a criminal law is subject to a fine, and/or a term in jail, or prison, depending on the type of crime. The potential for punishment as a result of violating a criminal law is called *CRIMINAL LIABILITY*. Some acts by security guard/proprietary private security officers for which criminal liability is possible include:

➢ *INTIMIDATION:*
Threatening physical harm or otherwise frightening people when they do not cooperate or confess to a crime.

➤ *EXCESSIVE PHYSICAL FORCE*:

Where an arrest is made, the law allows only the use of physical force, which is reasonable or necessary to restrain the suspect if he/she is resisting, in order to make the arrest. Where more force is used than that which the law allows, the arresting party is said to be using "excessive force" and may be held criminally as well as civilly liable. An example of excessive force is the discharge of a firearm in shooting a suspect in order to protect personal property. By law, deadly force is allowed only to protect lives.

➤ *USE OF UNAUTHORIZED DEADLY WEAPONS:*

Becoming registered as a security guard DOES NOT entitle a security guard to carry a weapon. Some weapons such as knives with blades longer then 2 inches or switch-blade knives, brass knuckles, nunchakus, or sawed-off shotguns cannot be carried by security guards. Security guards cannot carry a gun and/or a baton unless they have the additional exposed firearm permit and/or baton certificate. If they carry the gun concealed they must also have a concealed weapons permit issued by their local law enforcement agency.

Proprietary private security officers are unarmed and cannot carry a gun or a baton. Proprietary private security officers cannot carry any deadly weapons. Proprietary private security officer cannot carry weapons such as switchblade knives or knife's with blades over 2 inches in length, brass knuckles, nunchakus, batons, or guns as they are considered deadly weapons.

➤ *UNLAWFUL USE OF DEFENSIVE WEAPONS*:

Security guards cannot carry handguns and batons unless authorized by the Bureau. Security guards are allowed to carry an exposed firearm and/or baton only after the security guard completes the Bureau recognized training and the appropriate permits are issued.

➤ *FALSE ARREST*:

MISDEMEANOR ARREST - a private person making a misdemeanor arrest may be found criminally liable for a false arrest if the arrest is made and the arresting party did not actually observe the suspect commit the misdemeanor in his/her presence.

(Revised1 10/11)

FELONY ARREST - a private person making a felony arrest may be found criminally liable for a false arrest if the arrest is made or caused to be made by others and the arresting party does not have reasonable cause to believe that the person arrested committed the felony.

EVERYONE HAS CIVIL LIABILITY

The legal term *"PARTY"* can be a person, company, or organization.

When one party believes it has been injured, damaged, or wronged by another party, it may make a lawful claim for damages.

The claim or *"LAWSUIT"* is presented to a civil court where both parties may explain their positions to a judge or jury.

A court judge may decide whether or not one party in a lawsuit has damaged another.

If damages are due, the court will decide, after a trial, how much money must be paid by one party to another.

The responsibility for the things we do, or fail to do, with the possibility of being sued by another is called *"CIVIL LIABILITY."*

WHY IS YOUR EMPLOYER ALSO RESPONSIBLE FOR YOUR ACTIONS?

As a security guard/proprietary private security officer, you are a representative of your employer. Therefore, any negligence or wrongful acts committed by you may also cause your employer to be held responsible. Suits may be brought against you (the security guard/proprietary private security officer) and/or your employer.

FOR EXAMPLE:
A security guard/proprietary private security officer makes a false arrest. The person arrested may file a civil suit for damages against the security guard/proprietary private security officer, his employer, and all of those believed to be responsible.

Even if the civil suit against you (the security guard/proprietary private security officer) or your employer fails, the action may be costly for you and your employer to defend.

WHEN SHOULD A SECURITY GUARD/PROPRIETARY PRIVATE SECURITY OFFICER ARREST?

A security guard/proprietary private security officer who is expected to make arrests should receive explicit instructions and training on how to do so. Training should make clear the *circumstances* under which an arrest can be made and the *procedure* for making it, so as to minimize civil liability.

As a security guard/proprietary private security officer, you should work primarily in a preventive role. Use *good judgement* and *exercise caution* when faced with an arrest situation.

Every person must be accountable for his/her actions. Acts of a security guard or proprietary private security officer in an arrest situation are easy to defend when good judgement and good faith have been used. A security guard/proprietary private security officer must not be afraid to act in an arrest situation, but must use restraint and good judgment.

EXAM REVIEW NO. 7

NOW, on another sheet of paper, answer the following questions:

Q. 18 TELLING A SUSPECT "YOU'D BETTER START TALKING OR YOU'LL BE SORRY," IS AN EXAMPLE OF:

A. Intimidation
B. Excessive physical force

Q. 19 NO OTHER PERMIT IS REQUIRED TO CARRY A GUN IF YOU HAVE A SECURITY GUARD REGISTRATION, ALARM RESPONDERS REGISTRATION, PRIVATE INVESTIGATOR LICENSE OR PRIVATE PATROL OPERATOR LICENSE.

A. True
B. False

Q. 20 WHAT TYPE OF LIABILITY REFERS TO THE RIGHT A PARTY HAS TO
INITIATE A LAWSUIT?

A. Criminal liability
B. Civil liability

Q. 21 IF A SECURITY GUARD IS CHARGED WITH MAKING A FALSE ARREST,
WHAT TYPE OF LIABILITY IS INCURRED?

A. Criminal liability
B. Civil liability

PART G.

FACTORS TO CONSIDER BEFORE MAKING AN ARREST

ARE SECURITY GUARD/PROPRIETARY PRIVATE SECURITY OFFICERS REQUIRED TO MAKE ARRESTS?

At no time are you, as a security guard/proprietary private security officer, obligated to make an arrest. You may be at the scene when a violation occurs, but you do not have to make an arrest.

WHAT ARE YOU PRIMARY RESPONSIBILITIES?

Your first responsibility should be *prevention*. After a crime has been committed, your responsibility should be to *observe and report*.

The purpose of this training is not to encourage you to make more arrests (citizen arrests), but to teach you the law concerning arrests, so you will know what you can and cannot do under the law.

The above direction is a suggestion and is at the discretion of the employer. Some employers may want their security personnel to be more proactive as long as they stay within the parameters of what is lawful regarding private persons (citizen's) arrest.

WHAT FACTORS SHOULD YOU CONSIDER?

In addition to the law, there are other important factors you should consider before making an arrest. Here are a few:

1. *PHYSICAL SIZE.* Is the suspect bigger or stronger than you are? In better physical condition?

2. *WEAPONS.* Is the suspect armed? Could he/she be carrying a concealed weapon?

3. *ESCAPE.* If you do not make an arrest at this moment, will the suspect get away? Not just leave the scene - but get away completely? If you get a good description and call the police *WITHOUT DELAY*, the police may be able to make the arrest.

(Revised1 10/11)

4. *TYPE OF OFFENSE.* Is the offense major or minor? You should be more concerned with major offenses. A person setting fire on a loading dock is a more likely candidate for arrest than kids climbing a fence to steal apples from your employer's orchards.

5. *RELATION TO YOUR JOB.* Does the offense relate to property or persons you were hired to protect? As a good citizen, you want to uphold the law, but your first duty is to your employer. After all, your employer is paying you!

EXAM REVIEW NO. 8

NOW, on another sheet of paper, answer the following questions:

Q. 22 WHILE YOU ARE ON DUTY AT A SHOPPING CENTER, YOU SEE A 12-YEAR OLD JABBING AN ICE PICK INTO A PATRON'S CAR TIRES. YOU SHOULD *FIRST*:

A. Pick the 12-year old up and throw him/her out of the parking lot.
B. Get a good description and call the police.
C. Run at the 12-year old and yell so the child will run away.
D. Approach him/her and tell them to stop.

Q. 23 A MAN IS SMASHING TABLES AND CHAIRS AT A BAR YOU ARE SECURITY GUARD/PROPRIETARY PRIVATE SECURITY OFFICERING. HE IS ABOUT 6' 8" AND WEIGHS 280 LBS. YOU SHOULD:

A. Consider your safety and the safety of others.
B. Request patrons of the bar to clear the area.
C. Call the police for assistance.
D. Take all of the measures above.

Q. 24 YOU ARE SECURITY GUARD/PROPRIETARY PRIVATE SECURITY WORKING IN A JEWELRY STORE AT CLOSING TIME. THE LAST PATRON HAS LEFT AND YOUR EMPLOYER IS ABOUT TO LOCK UP. YOU NOTICE A MAN SITTING IN A CAR AND THE MOTOR IS RUNNING. YOU CLEARLY SEE HE HAS A GUN IN HIS HAND. YOU SHOULD *FIRST:*

A. Run out to the car and tell him to freeze.
B. Have the owner call the police and get a description and vehicle license number if possible.
C. Walk to the car and order the man to leave.

Q. 25 YOU ARE WORKING AT A CLUB WHERE EVERYTHING IS QUIET. DOWN THE STREET TWO MEN GET INTO A FIGHT. YOU SHOULD:

A. Stay where you are. You have been hired to guard the dance. You could call the police if it doesn't involve leaving your post.
B. Call someone over to watch the dance while you go down the street to break up the fight.
C. Shout down the street for the men to break it up.

Q. 26 YOU ARE PATROLLING A SHOPPING AREA WHEN YOU SEE A JUVENILE RIDING A SKATEBOARD. YOU KNOW THAT SKATING IS AGAINST THE MALL POLICY. YOUR BEST COURSE OF ACTION WOULD BE TO:

A. Handle the matter formally as a criminal offense.
B. Politely approach the boy and inform him of shopping mall policy regarding skating in the mall.

The above direction is a suggestion and is at the discretion of the employer. Some employers may want their security personnel to be more proactive as long as they stay within the parameters of what is lawful regarding private persons (citizen's) arrest.

PART H

ARRESTABLE OFFENSES

WHAT ARE THE THREE CATEGORIES OF ARRESTABLE OFFENSES?

The Penal Code defines criminal offenses. This program will not attempt to cover all of them, but will cover many of the most common ones. The Penal Code classifies crimes into three categories: *Infractions, Misdemeanors, and Felonies.*

INFRACTIONS

Infractions are offenses that are punishable only by a modest monetary fine. There is normally no jail sentence imposed for committing an offense, which is defined as an infraction, and the person committing the offense is normally cited at the scene in a fashion similar to the issuance of a traffic citation. The offender is normally not taken into custody or arrested but merely detained for purposes of issuing the citation. For the most part, infractions are reserved for specified traffic violations such as speeding (California Vehicle Code §40000.1), though other statutes impose infraction penalties as well (smoking on public transportation, Health and Safety Code §25949.8; littering public property, Penal Code §374.4.) Because most infractions occur on public property, public highways and roadways, or in areas not routinely patrolled by private security, most security guard/proprietary private security officers will not be confronted with situations involving the violations of laws which carry infraction penalties. Nor are private security guards/proprietary private security officers normally authorized to issue citations, commonly known as notices to appear in court. For this reason, enforcement of laws involving infractions are usually reserved for law enforcement officers.

MISDEMEANORS

Misdemeanors are offenses that are punishable by a fine and/or term in the county jail. The following two conditions must exist in order for you to arrest a person on a misdemeanor charge:

1. The misdemeanor must have been *attempted* or *committed*.

2. It must have taken place (happened) *in your presence*.

The following are common misdemeanors (PC stands for Penal Code):

> ➤ ASSAULT — (§240 PC) An unlawful *attempt* coupled with the present ability to commit a violent injury upon the person of another.

> ➤ BATTERY — (§242 PC) Any willful and unlawful use of force or violence upon another person.

> ➤ DISTURBING THE PEACE — (§415 PC) Unlawfully fighting in a public place or challenging to fight; malicious and willful disturbances of another by loud and unreasonable noise; using offensive words to provoke a violent reaction.

> ➤ INDECENT EXPOSURE — (§314 PC) The act of exposing the person or private parts thereof in any public place where other persons may be offended.

> ➤ LITTERING — (§374 PC) Throwing waste matter in a place other than designated containers.

> ➤ PETTY THEFT — (§488 PC) The taking of property of a value of $950.00 or less (this is often the case in shoplifting.)

> ➤ TRESPASSING — (§602 PC) Entering posted property without permission. Damaging or destroying property, or refusing to leave when asked by the owner or his agent.

> ➤ VANDALISM — (§594 PC) Maliciously defacing, damaging, or destroying property.

FELONIES

A *felony* is a more serious offense that is punishable by a sentence of death, imprisonment in a jail or prison, and/or a fine.

The following two conditions must exist in order to arrest a person on a felony charge:

1. The felony *must have been committed*.
2. A reasonable cause must exist to believe that the person being arrested actually committed the crime. Such reasonable cause must be based on evidence linking the person to the crime. Examples of such evidence may include physical evidence such as articles of clothing belonging to the suspect and left at the scene of the crime, or testimonial evidence such as observations by the security guard/proprietary private security officer or by other persons which are told to the security guard/proprietary private security officer in which the suspect was observed committing the crime.

The following are common felonies (PC stands for Penal Code):

➢ ASSAULT WITH A
    DEADLY WEAPON   (§245 PC) Assault of a person by another with a deadly weapon or instrument or by any means of force likely to produce great bodily injury.

➢ ARSON   (§451 PC) The willful and unlawful setting of a fire.

➢ GRAND THEFT   (§487 PC) The taking of money, labor, or real or personal property of a value exceeding $950.00 or the taking of property *from the person of another*.

➢ BURGLARY   (§459 PC) The entering of the residence or property of another with the *intent* to commit grand theft, petty theft, or any felony.

➢ KIDNAPPING   (§207 PC) Taking and transporting a person against his will.

➢ ROBBERY   (§211 PC) By force or intimidation, taking personal property from a person or from the immediate presence of a person against that person's will

➤ RAPE	(§261 PC) Forcing sexual intercourse.
➤ MANSLAUGHTER	(§192 PC) The unlawful killing of another human being includes voluntary, involuntary, or vehicular manslaughter.
➤ MURDER	(§187 PC) The unlawful killing of another human being with malice and forethought.

EXAM REVIEW NO. 9

NOW, on another sheet of paper, answer the following questions:
Identify the following crimes, based on the definitions you have just learned.

Q. 27 TWO MEN GRAB AN EMPLOYEE GETTING OUT OF HIS/HER CAR IN THE PARKING LOT. THEY SHOVE THE EMPLOYEE INTO THEIR CAR AND START DRIVING AWAY. THIS MAY BE:

A. Kidnapping, a felony.
B. Robbery, a felony.

Q. 28 A FAMILY RETURNS HOME TO DISCOVER THEIR HOUSEHOLD FURNISHINGS ARE MISSING. THEY MAY BE VICTIMS OF:

A. Burglary, a felony.
B. Robbery, a felony.

Q. 29 AN EX-EMPLOYEE OF A SUPERMARKET WAITS IN HER CAR UNTIL THE MANAGER CLOSES THE BUILDING AND WALKS TOWARDS HIS CAR. SHE STEPS OUT OF HER CAR, POINTS A GUN AT THE MANAGER, AND FIRES THREE SHOTS, KILLING THE MANAGER. WHAT CRIME MAY HAVE BEEN COMMITTED?

A. Arson, a felony.
B. Murder, a felony.

Q. 30 TOM IS ANGERED BECAUSE JIM WAS DANCING WITH TOM'S GIRLFRIEND. TOM WAITS OUTSIDE THE DOOR WITH A LARGE BOARD HE PICKED UP FROM A CONSTRUCTION SITE. WHEN JIM COMES OUT OF THE BUILDING, TOM SWINGS THE BOARD AND HITS JIM IN THE FACE. THIS IS:

A. Assault with a deadly weapon, a felony.
B. Battery, a misdemeanor.

Q. 31 SECRETARIES LINDA AND JUDY GET INTO AN ARGUMENT OVER PAY RAISES. SECRETARY JUDY LEAVES THE ARGUMENT TO GO TO THE REST ROOM. SECRETARY LINDA, STILL ANGRY, HIDES BEHIND A LARGE BOOKCASE. AS JUDY RETURNS, LINDA TRIES TO TOPPLE THE BOOKCASE ONTO JUDY. THE BOOKCASE BARELY MISSES HER. THIS IS:

A. Assault, a misdemeanor
B. Assault with a deadly weapon, a felony.
C. Either A or B

Q. 32 A MAN WHO HAS PURCHASED A NEW $975.00 LAWN MOWER PUSHES IT OUT TO HIS CAR AND LEAVES IT BESIDE THE TRUNK WHILE HE GOES BACK INTO THE STORE TO GET A SACK OF FERTILIZER. WHILE HE IS GONE, SOMEONE DRIVES UP IN A STATION WAGON, PUTS THE NEW LAWN MOWER IN THE BACK OF THE WAGON, AND DRIVES OFF. WHAT CRIME IS THIS?

A. Robbery, a felony.
B. Grand theft, a felony.

Q. 33 A MAN IS SITTING IN THE LOBBY OF AN AUTOMOBILE SHOWROOM. AT 5:00 P.M. THE SECURITY OFFICER STARTS TO LOCK UP FOR THE NIGHT AND ASKS THE MAN TO LEAVE. THE MAN REFUSES, SO THE SECURITY OFFICER ASKS IF THE MAN IS WAITING FOR SOMEONE. THE MAN REPLIES, "NONE OF YOUR BUSINESS." AGAIN, THE SECURITY OFFICER ASKS THE MAN TO LEAVE. HE REFUSES. THE MAN HAS COMMITTED THE CRIME OF:

A. Trespassing, a misdemeanor.
B. Disturbing the peace, a misdemeanor.

Q. 34 AN ANGRY EMPLOYEE POURS LIGHTER FLUID IN A TRASH CONTAINER IN THE STOCK ROOM, THEN LIGHTS IT WITH A MATCH. THIS IS:

A. Vandalism, a misdemeanor.
B. Arson, a felony.

Q. 35 YOU DRIVE UP TO A STORE AT 2:00 A.M. AND OBSERVE TWO MEN BREAKING OPEN A DOOR AND BEGINNING TO LOAD A PICKUP TRUCK WITH MERCHANDISE. WHEN THEY SEE YOU, THEY TURN AND RUN. THIS IS:

A. Burglary, a felony.
B. Robbery, a felony.

PART I.

PRIVATE PERSONS ARREST

Although your normal responsibilities include the *preventing* of problems and *observation* of detail after an offense, there may be rare occasions when you consider it necessary to *arrest*. Every company in the private security industry has different policies about when and if you should *arrest*. *If you don't know your company's policy, find out.*

A security guard/proprietary private security officer's legal powers to arrest are *no greater than those of any other private citizen*. An arrest made by such a private party is commonly known as a *"citizen's arrest."*

According to the Penal Code Section 834, "An arrest is taking a person into custody in a manner authorized by law." Penal Code Section 834 also goes on to state that, "An arrest may be made by a peace officer or by a private person."

Penal Code Section 837 specifies the *conditions* under which you, as a private person, may make an arrest. "A private person may arrest another.

1. For a public offense committed or attempted in his presence.

2. When the person arrested has committed a felony, although not in his presence.

3. When a felony has been, in fact, committed and he has reasonable cause for believing the person arrested to have committed it."

In making your decision to arrest someone, you must *first determine whether the offense is a felony or a misdemeanor.*

EXAMPLE OF A MISDEMEANOR OFFENSE

If you observed a person picking up a rock and throwing it through a plate glass window, that person could be arrested. Breaking a window is a misdemeanor offense and you know that he committed the offense because *you saw the person do it.*

On the other hand, consider this case: You hear a plate glass window break and rush to the front of the building only to see a group of teenagers laughing and milling around. Two of them point to one of the others and say, "He did it." In this instance, you would not have grounds for an arrest. It appears an offense has been committed, but you did not actually see the person doing it.

REMEMBER:

To arrest someone for the commission of a misdemeanor, the offense must be:

1) committed in your presence; or 2) attempted *in your presence*!

EXAMPLE OF A FELONY OFFENSE

You are patrolling an apartment complex and you see an apartment door open. You look inside and see that the place has been burglarized. As you leave the apartment, you see two men carrying large bundles of assorted valuables to a waiting van. They see you and speed up. You call for them to halt, but they load up the van and are in the process of getting into the front seat. You are justified in questioning these men.

On the other hand, consider this: You are told by an apartment dweller that he was just burglarized and you see two men walking towards a van with the motor running. The men look around suspiciously but are carrying nothing. You should get descriptions and *observe and report.*

REMEMBER:

To arrest someone for committing a felony, 1) the felony must have been committed and 2) you must have reasonable cause for believing that the person you are arresting actually committed the felony.

EXAM REVIEW NO. 10

NOW, on another sheet of paper, answer the following questions:

Analyze the following incidents and decide if you have grounds for arrest.

Q. 36 YOU ARE MAKING YOUR ROUNDS AT A SHOPPING CENTER AND COME TO A PICKUP TRUCK PARKED AT THE CURB. IN THE BACK OF THE TRUCK ARE TWO COLOR TV SETS STILL IN THEIR PACKING BOXES. THE TWO MEN IN THE TRUCK LOOK SUSPICIOUS. ACCORDING TO THE LAW YOU CAN ARREST THESE TWO MEN.

    A. True
    B. False

Q.37 YOU ARE ON DUTY AS A SECURITY GUARD/PROPRIETARY PRIVATE SECURITY OFFICER AT A FACTORY AND YOU OBSERVE A SUSPECT POURING WHAT APPEARS TO BE GASOLINE ON THE GROUND NEXT TO SOME STORAGE TANKS. AS YOU APPROACH, HE LIGHTS A MATCH AND THROWS IT ON THE LIQUID, IGNITING IT. ACCORDING TO THE LAW YOU CAN ARREST THIS MAN.

    A. True
    B. False

Q. 38 ACCORDING TO THE LAW, WHICH OF THE FOLLOWING CONDITIONS MUST EXIST BEFORE YOU CAN MAKE A MISDEMEANOR ARREST?

    A. The suspect must admit to the crime.
    B. The crime must have been committed or attempted in your presence.
    C. Someone told you the suspect did it.

Q. 39 ACCORDING TO THE LAW, WHICH OF THE FOLLOWING CONDITIONS MUST EXIST BEFORE YOU CAN MAKE A FELONY ARREST?

    A. The felony must have been committed and you have reason to believe the person you are arresting actually committed it.
    B. You think a crime has been committed and the person you are arresting is the only person around.
    C. A citizen tells you he thinks someone was just assaulted.

PART J.

MAKING AN ARREST

THE SUSPECT

According to our legal system, a person is innocent until proven guilty. It is up to the court to decide if a person is guilty - not the police, not the district attorney, and not a private person. When a person is arrested, that person is called a *suspect*. The person is then considered a suspect until the court finds the person guilty or innocent. Therefore, do not refer to an arrested person as the *"criminal," "offender," "robber," "murderer," "burglar,"* or by any other term which implies guilt. You can say *"he," "she," "they," "this person,"* or *"the suspect"* since none of these terms imply guilt.

MAKING AN ARREST

If you should happen to be in a situation where a citizen arrest is called for, you should tell the person that he/she is under citizen's arrest and what the charges are, and your authority to make the citizen's arrest. Once you say "You are under arrest for burglary," the suspect may or may not cooperate. If the suspect resists and tries to escape, you must then decide whether or not to use reasonable force. You may ask as many persons as you think necessary to help you in making the arrest.

USE OF FORCE IN AN ARREST

If a suspect resists arrest, you are allowed to use reasonable force to subdue the suspect. Reasonable force is that degree of force that is not excessive and is appropriate in protecting oneself or one's property. If the suspect submits willingly, no force is necessary. If a suspect should resist arrest, remember that the only force allowed is that which is reasonable and necessary to overcome the resistance.

WHAT IS EXCESSIVE FORCE?

Examples of excessive force include knocking unconscious an unarmed suspect when he is only trying to leave the scene. Handcuffs may be used on persons who have resisted or on suspects you think may be trying to resist or escape.

WHAT IS DETAINMENT?

A person who voluntarily responds to questioning and is not actually restrained (i.e., free to go at any time) is considered to be *detained*. A person may be detained by the police for further questioning in an investigation, and that person is not necessarily under arrest. The police have the authority to detain a person against his/her will and still not arrest that person. Security guard/proprietary private security officers *do not* have the authority to detain a person against their will except under **Penal Code Section 490.5**, which is covered in detail further on in the study manual. (***MERCHANTS PRIVILEGE RULE, PART L***)

WHEN IS A SUSPECT CONSIDERED TO BE UNDER ARREST?

It should be clear to the suspect that he/she is under arrest *after* you have told the suspect of your *intention, cause, and authority* to arrest him/her. However, there are also other actions that may make a suspect feel he/she is under arrest. If, because of your uniform, badge, hat, or verbal actions, the suspect concludes he/she must answer your questions or is not free to walk away, he/she may justifiably claim he was under arrest.

WHAT IS THE RIGHT WAY TO APPROACH SUSPECTS?

Guilt by association is not a lawful way to make arrests. Let's look at an example:

It is 11:00 p.m. and a security guard/proprietary private security officer is making his/her rounds of the plant when he finds Gate No. 5 open. There are pry marks on the chain that normally holds the gate shut. About 50 yards from the gate is an old pickup truck parked by the side of the road. The hood is up, and two men are bent over looking at the motor. The proprietary security officer proprietary walks over and says, "All right, you guys. What are you doing here?" One of the men responds by saying, "What's it to you pal?" The security guard/proprietary private security officer answers angrily, "Look, you better tell me what you're doing here or you're in trouble!" Neither man replies. One of them gets into the driver's seat and turns over the engine. The proprietary security officer proprietary then asks, "Didn't you hear what I said?" The other man says, "Leave us alone." The proprietary security officer proprietary moves to the front of the truck and grabs the man's arm, stating, "You guys aren't going anywhere until you answer a few questions."

ANALYSIS

Finding the gate open with pry marks on the chain does not necessarily mean that a crime has been committed. There are a number of possible explanations short of forced entry. Next, there is nothing to tie the two men to forcing the gate open except that their truck was parked nearby. The security guard/proprietary private security officer cannot demand that the men answer his questions. The security guard/proprietary private security officer's attitude, tone of voice, uniform, and badge could easily have made the men believe that they were being arrested. If the security guard/proprietary private security officer refused to let them leave and if it turned out they had nothing to do with forcing the gate, the men could sue the security guard/proprietary private security officer for false arrest and for battery, because the security guard/proprietary private security officer grabbed the man's arm.

WHAT THE SECURITY GUARD/PROPRIETARY PRIVATE SECURITY OFFICER SHOULD HAVE DONE

First, he/she should have examined the condition of the gate carefully, recorded the license number of the truck, and obtained a description of the two men. Next, the security guard/proprietary private security officer should have secured the gate and reported its condition to his/her supervisor, being careful to watch for other suspicious activity. The security guard/proprietary private security officer may or may not decide to talk with the two men. He might enter into a friendlier conversation with them by asking if they had seen anyone near the gate. If they are not cooperative, there is nothing the security guard/proprietary private security officer can do except observe closely. The security guard/proprietary private security officer should never touch another person except when reasonable force is necessary when placing that person under citizen's arrest.

The above direction is a suggestion and is at the discretion of the employer. Some employers may want their security personnel to be more proactive as long as they stay within the parameters of what is lawful regarding private persons (citizen's) arrest.

A BETTER APPROACH

Remember the part about friendly conversation? Although you cannot demand answers from a person, you can always engage them in casual conversation. Here is a better approach:

> "Hi! Got car troubles?" One of the men replies, "Yeah! This darn thing shorts out every once in a while." The security guard/proprietary private security officer then asks, "Say, have you seen anybody around the gate?" The men reply, "No, we haven't seen anyone except you." The security guard/proprietary private security officer says, "How long have you been here?" "Oh, maybe five minutes." "Well, thanks for your help. If you need to call for road service, I can make the call for you." "Thanks anyway, but we'll get it going." The security guard/proprietary private security officer then walks away.

The security guard/proprietary private security officer may not have gotten much information, but at least he/she had a chance to observe each man closely and check their activities without running the risk of bad public relations or a false-citizen's arrest suit.

EXAM REVIEW NO. 11

NOW, on another sheet of paper, answer the following questions:

Q. 40   WHAT SHOULD YOU SAY TO A PERSON YOU ARE ARRESTING FOR BURGLARY?

    A. State your intent to arrest.
    B. State the charge, which is suspicion of burglary.
    C. State your authority to make the arrest.
    D. All of the above.

Q. 41   ONCE YOU DETAIN A PERSON AGAINST HIS WILL, YOU HAVE PLACED THAT PERSON UNDER CITIZEN'S ARREST.

    A. True
    B. False

Q. 42   IF YOU ARE STRUGGLING WITH A SUSPECT IN TRYING TO GET THE SUSPECT UNDER CONTROL AND THERE ARE A NUMBER OF BYSTANDERS, WHAT DOES THE LAW SAY YOU CAN DO?

    A. Ask the bystanders to help you.
    B. Demand that the bystanders help you.
    C. Demand the bystanders call the police.

Q. 43   UNDER WHAT CONDITIONS MAY *"REASONABLE FORCE"* BE USED AGAINST A SUSPECT?

    A. Protection of self.
    B. Protection of others.
    C. To overcome suspect resistance.
    D. Any of the above.

PART K.

<u>SEARCHING THE SUSPECT</u>

You should avoid searching a suspect. Laws protect the rights of suspects who are being searched. This section explains what you should and should not do.

You are not allowed to search someone in order to find evidence for making a citizen's arrest.

When you see someone steal something you have been hired to protect, you may first detain the person by telling him/her that they are under arrest for theft. Then you may physically detain the person for the police to search. You should not give the suspect an opportunity to dispose of any items taken.

If you have reasonable cause to believe you are in physical danger by detaining the suspect, you may search the individual for weapons.

REMEMBER

> You may search for only *one* thing – **WEAPONS (Penal Code §846).**

METHOD OF "FRISK" SEARCHING FOR WEAPONS

> A frisk is nothing more than a *quick check* to see if a suspect has a concealed weapon. This should occur after the suspect is arrested. To frisk a suspect, follow these steps:
>
> A. Stand behind the suspect
> B. Run your hands over the outside of their clothing
> C. Pat those areas where a weapon might be concealed
> D. Remove anything that feels like a weapon

CAUTION

> Do not remove any article that does not feel like a weapon.

IMPORTANT

Always use discretion when touching a suspect. When ever possible have a security guard/proprietary private security officer of the same sex conduct the frisk, and always try to have witnesses to the frisk. ***STAY ALERT!*** Don't relax after a frisk or take your eyes off the suspect after you have completed the frisk. They may still have a weapon you did not find!

The frisk should be done quickly, and if possible, with another security guard/proprietary private security officer standing by. Practice the frisk on a partner by having him/her conceal a small object. During a frisk, you may also discover illegal items called *contraband*. The most common type of contraband is narcotics. If you discover contraband while you are frisking for concealed weapons, leave it alone and tell the police when they arrive.

EXAM REVIEW NO. 12

NOW, on another sheet of paper, answer the following questions:

Q. 44 ACCORDING TO THE TEXT, YOU SHOULD:

A. Not search a suspect unless you have reason to believe he/she has a weapon.
B. Search all suspects immediately.
C. Search only persons suspected of major crimes.
D. Search only those persons with a police record.

Q. 45 WHAT MUST YOU DO BEFORE YOU FRISK A SUSPECT?

A. Handcuff the suspect.
B. Arrest the suspect.
C. Tie the suspect's hands over his head.
D. Write you a report.

Q. 46 A FRISK BY A SECURITY GUARD/PROPRIETARY PRIVATE SECURITY OFFICER IS A SEARCH FOR:

A. Weapons only.
B. Stolen property only.
C. Weapons or stolen property.
D. Anything.

ILLUSTRATION OF THE FRISK

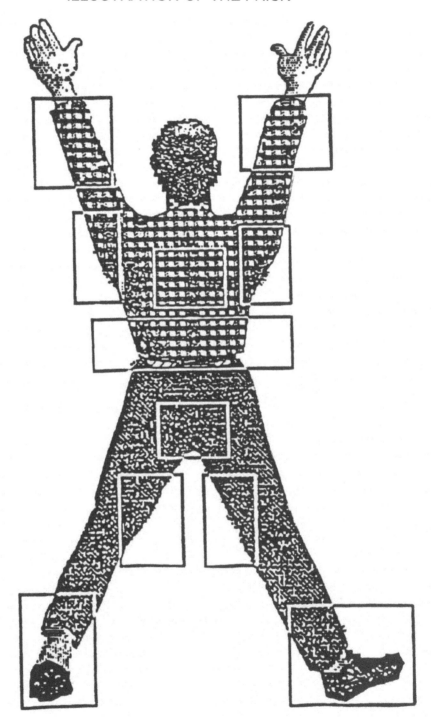

PART L.

SEARCHING A SUSPECT UNDER THE MERCHANT'S PRIVILEGE RULE

The Merchant's Privilege Rule is found in the California Penal Code Section 490.5. Subdivisions (f) and (g) of this statute provide legal authority for a merchant or their employee or agent, including a security officer, to detain persons suspected of shoplifting in a retail store. In part, the law states:

"(f)(1) A merchant may detain a person for a reasonable time for the purpose of conducting an investigation in a reasonable manner whenever the merchant has probable cause to believe the person to be detained is attempting to unlawfully take or has unlawfully taken merchandise from the merchant's premises.

(2) In making the detention a merchant may use a reasonable amount of non-deadly force necessary to protect himself or herself and to prevent escape of the person detained or the loss of property.

(3) During the period of detention any items which a merchant has probable cause to believe were unlawfully taken from the premises of the merchant and which are in plain view may be examined by the merchant for purposes of ascertaining the ownership thereof.

(4) A merchant or an agent thereof, having probable cause to believe the person detained was attempting to unlawfully take or has taken any item from the premises, may request the person detained to voluntarily surrender the item. Should the person detained refuse to surrender the item of which there is probable cause to believe has been unlawfully taken from the premises, or attempted to be unlawfully taken from the premises, a limited and reasonable search may be conducted by those authorized to make the detention in order to recover the item. Only packages, shopping bags, handbags or other property in the immediate possession of the person detained, but not including any clothing worn by the person, may be searched pursuant to this subdivision. Upon surrender or discovery of the item, the person detained may also be requested, but may not be required, to provide adequate proof of his or her true identity."

The important things to remember when working for a retail merchant are:

1.   That a suspected shoplifter can be detained where there is reasonable cause to believe that the suspect has unlawfully taken or attempted to take an item from the store. This is not an arrest, but merely a detention in order to investigate further the reasonable belief that a theft has occurred or was attempted.

2.   That reasonable *non-deadly* force may be used to carryout the detention where the suspect resists.

3.   That following a request to surrender the item believed taken, you may search their belongings (limited to shopping bags, handbags, and other items) in the immediate possession of the suspect, *but not a search of clothing or apparel worn by the suspect.*

4.   That following the detention, and if it is established that shoplifting has occurred or was attempted, and if criminal charges are to be pursued, the suspect must be given over to law enforcement authorities. This must occur within a reasonable period of time following detention.

5.   Mall security personnel should be very aware of the fact that they protect mall property and that the individual stores in that mall are privately owned and rent space from the mall owners. With this in mind, unless the mall owners have a signed agreement with the stores that the security department in the mall have the permission to act as individual store security, security personnel may not use Penal Code Section 490.5 inside individual stores.

PART M.

AFTER THE ARREST

WHAT SHOULD A SECURITY GUARD/PROPRIETARY PRIVATE SECURITY OFFICER DO AFTER AN ARREST?

After you arrest someone, you must *turn him or her over to the police WITHOUT DELAY.* You should *write down the time* you (1) made the arrest, and (2) called the police. If you delay too long in calling the police, you may be guilty of an illegal detention even though you might have spent the time questioning the suspect.

WHAT IS REASONABLE DELAY?

Reasonable delays, however, are usually acceptable. For example, if you had to walk a half-mile to get to the nearest phone or wait at your post for your partner to relieve you, these would be considered reasonable delays. However, if a phone is handy and you wait an hour before calling, this could be considered an unreasonable delay.

WHAT IS THE PEACE OFFICERS RESPONSIBILITY?

The police upon arrival at the scene will evaluate the elements of the crime, detention, and arrest. They will then make the determination as to whether they must take custody of the person from the security guard/proprietary private security officer. If the elements of the crime that the person was arrested for have not been legally met, the officer could simply release the person and leave the scene after giving the security guard/proprietary private security officer an explanation.

If you have made a legal arrest, the police, by law, must take custody of the suspect. *Custody* means "to take charge of." If the suspect is charged with a serious offense, the police will probably take him/her down to the station to take fingerprints and make photo identification. Also, they might not release the suspect unless bail is posted.

Taking custody of suspects charged with less serious offenses may not involve going to the police station. The police may choose simply to cite and release the suspect pending a hearing. This is also considered "taking into custody." The police will take down a statement of what happened, so you should take care to observe as many factual details as possible. The police will also investigate to collect evidence. You may also be asked to testify at the trial.

RELEASE FROM CUSTODY

If the peace officer decides to release the suspect, Penal Code Section 849 (c) provides that the peace officer shall include a record of release in the report. Thereafter, such arrest shall not be deemed an arrest, but detention only (Penal Code §849.5).

PRIVATE PERSON'S ARREST - MISDEMEANOR

If the suspect is charged with a misdemeanor (such as trespassing, petty theft, or disturbing the peace), *you will be recorded as the person making the arrest.* You cannot arrest a suspect for a misdemeanor unless you *actually see a violation happen.*

If you arrest a suspect, you must call the police. When they arrive, turn the suspect over to them and make your statement.

Other things you may be expected to do if you make a misdemeanor arrest include:

1. Meeting with the district attorney (usually the next day) to discuss the case and give a sworn statement regarding what happened.

2. Attending the suspect's hearing.

3. Testifying at the suspect's trial.

EXAM REVIEW NO. 13

NOW, on another sheet of paper, answer the following questions:

Q. 47 HOW SOON MUST YOU TURN A SUSPECT OVER TO THE PEACE OFFICER AFTER AN ARREST?

    A. With out delay.
    B. At any time.
    C. After reporting to your supervisor.

Q. 48 IT WOULD BE LAWFUL IF YOU HELD A SUSPECT FOR TWO HOURS SO YOUR SUPERVISOR COULD QUESTION HIM/HER BEFORE YOU CALLED THE POLICE.

    A. True
    B. False

Q. 49 IF YOU HAVE MADE A LAWFUL ARREST, THE LOCAL PEACE OFFICER:

    A. Must take custody of the suspect only if the crime is a felony.
    B. Must take custody of the suspect only if the crime is a misdemeanor.
    C. Must take custody of the suspect regardless of whether the crime is a misdemeanor or a felony.
    D. Can refuse to take custody of the suspect.

Q. 50 IF THE CRIME COMMITTED IS A FELONY, WHO WILL MAKE THE ARREST?

    A. A proprietary private security guard/proprietary private security officer.
    B. The police.
    C. Either A or B.

Q. 51 WHAT WILL PROBABLY BE REQUIRED OF YOU AFTER MAKING AN ARREST?

    A. Meeting with the district attorney.
    B. Attending the suspect's hearing.
    C. Testifying at the suspect's trial.
    D. All of the above.

PART N.

TERRORISM

WHAT IS TERRORISM?

Terrorism is the use of force or violence against persons or property in violation of the criminal laws of the Unites States for purposes of intimidation, coercion, or ransom. Terrorists often use threats to create fear among the public, to try to convince citizens that their government is powerless in preventing terrorism, and to get immediate publicity for their causes.

TYPES OF TERRORISM

All acts of terrorism are crimes. The Federal Bureau of Investigation (FBI) categorizes terrorism in the United States as one of two types - domestic terrorism or international terrorism.

Domestic Terrorism involves groups or individuals whose terrorist activities are directed at elements of our government or population without foreign direction.

International Terrorism involves groups or individuals whose terrorist activities are foreign based and/or directed by countries or groups outside the United States or whose activities transcend national boundaries.

NATURE AND CHARACTERISTICS OF TERRORISM

Terrorists look for visible targets where they can avoid detection before or after an attack such as international airports, large cities, major international events, resorts, and high-profile landmarks. Terrorist actions are well planned and are usually executed without any deviation to their plan. It is also theatrical, creating specific reactions from the audience (population). The terrorist will always stage and even rehearse their plan at least three times before perpetrating their actual attack. Terrorism is directed against governments, businesses, communities, and individuals. It may be perpetrated for the retaliation of perceived injustices to cause confrontation between parties; improve a bargaining position; or to demonstrate strength, commitment, and resolve.

Prior to a number of terrorist attacks, the perpetrators have been observed by security personnel and even recorded on surveillance cameras. However, since terrorists didn't enter the facility or building, in each case security chose to ignore them. Some terrorists have been observed taking photographs and making sketches of the site, yet security personnel hadn't felt it important to stop or question them. Some terrorist devices such as vehicles containing explosive devices had even been cited for parking in a "No Parking Zone" yet they had not investigated or determined its ownership. Remember, a terrorist will not usually attack unless they believe that their operation will be 100% successful.

Terrorists want media coverage to ensure that many people know about their activities. Some will even telephone the media just prior to, or even from their target, after they have taken control. That is why they select high-visibility targets and attempt to do maximum damage. They want a "High Body Count." Terrorists hope that attention will increase the public's fear, cause a planned government reaction, or attract sympathy to their cause.

While you cannot prevent deranged individuals or fanatics from plotting against their targets, the security guard/proprietary private security officer can minimize the terrorists' efforts with solid preparation and by just doing the job they have been paid to do. Whether a threat or an actual attack, it is the security guard/proprietary private security officer who is on the front line. They are usually the first to arrive at the scene; to size up (observe) the situation; the first to request (report) the necessary emergency response; the first to take control of the situation; the first to administer first aid until the emergency agencies arrive; and the first to advise the responding agencies of the specific details of the situation.

COUNTER TERRORIST TECHNIQUES OF PHYSICAL SECURITY

➢ **Deter** - Deterring terrorists activity by the hardening of the target, so that the terrorist does not have a 100% chance of success. They include the following: checking identifications, packages, and vehicles before they enter a secured area, making patrols or routes of travel unpredictable, and maintaining confidentiality.

➢ **Delay** - The use of barriers, locks, a response force and the controlling of vehicular access.

➢ **Deny** - Deny the terrorists the use of widespread panic and media leverage, which they attempt to exploit.

➢ **Detect** - Detection of terrorist activity can be accomplished through the analysis of threat intelligence. It can also occur by conducting entry searches, using detection equipment (x-ray, metal explosive), and closed circuit television.

(Revised1 10/11)

EXAM REVIEW NO. 14

Now, on another sheet of paper, answer the following questions:

Q. 52 Terrorism is a use of force or violence against persons or property for the purpose of intimidation or coercion.

    A. True
    B. False

Q. 53 All acts of terrorism are crimes?

    A. True
    B. False

Q. 54 What are the two types of terrorism?

    A. Chemical and Biological terrorism
    B. Computer and Sabotage
    C. Coercion and Fear
    D. Domestic and International

Q. 55 What are the characteristics of a terrorist?

    A. They will have a specific objective in mind.
    B. They will always conduct a surveillance of the target.
    C. They will rehearse their operation.
    D. All of the above.

Q. 56 A terrorist almost always acts with a specific objective in mind.

    A. True
    B. False

Q. 57 What are the four counter terrorist techniques of physical security?

    A. Security, weapons, deadly force and threat intelligence.
    B. Deter, delay, deny and detect.
    C. Deadly force, minimum force, de-escalation of force and entry searches.
    D. None of the above.

Q. 58 Terrorist actions are well planned and are usually executed without any deviation to their plan.

    A. True
    B. False

Q. 59 Terrorism is directed against governments, businesses, communities, and individuals.

    A. True
    B. False

PART O.

PROFESSIONAL CONDUCT OF A SECURITY GUARD/PROPRIETARY PRIVATE SECURITY OFFICER

The ability of the security guard/proprietary private security officers to fulfill their duties is dependent upon securing and maintaining public respect and approval, which includes obtaining the public's willingness to cooperate in the task of preventing crime. The extent to which the community's respect and trust can be secured is diminished when a security guard/proprietary private security officer acts in an unprofessional or unlawful manner. The personal conduct of a security guard/proprietary private security officer is always under a microscope. You must be constantly mindful of your obligations to serve your employer efficiently and effectively. The degree to which the community will cooperate with you is dependent upon its respect for, and confidence in you.

REMEMBER

The general public sometimes thinks of security guard/proprietary private security officers as police officers, due to the fact that their uniforms are not readily identifiable from a distance. As such, the security guard/proprietary private security officer should maintain his/her appearance and demeanor to the highest level.

(Revised1 10/11)

EXAM REVIEW NO. 15

Now, on another sheet of paper, answer the following questions:

Q. 60 Appearance and cleanliness are not as important as showing up on time for work.

   A. True
   B. False

Q. 61 The general public judges a security guard/proprietary private security officer by:

   A. Appearance
   B. Speech
   C. Attitude
   D. All of the above

Q. 62 Security guard/proprietary private security officers are peace officers while on duty.

   A. True
   B. False

Q. 63 Accepting gratuity is acceptable at certain times.

   A. True
   B. False

Q. 64 The ability of a private security company and its security officers to fulfill their duties is dependent upon securing and maintaining public respect and approval.

   A. True
   B. False

THIS IS THE END OF THE STUDY MANUAL

1. Look over the entire study manual one more time. Take note of the major sections, Part A through O.
2. Double-check your answers to the *CHECKUP QUESTIONS*.
3. Check your answers with the *Answers* to the Study Questions beginning on the next page.
4. Begin the final examination, marking your answers on the answer sheet provided.

PART P.

ANSWERS TO STUDY QUESTIONS

Part A: ROLE AND RESPONSIBILITIES OF THE SECURITY GUARD /PROPRIETARY PRIVATE SECURITY OFFICER

Exam Review #1:   **1.** B   **2.** B   **3.** C   **4.** D

Exam Review #2:   **5.** B   **6.** B

Part B: RELATIONS WITH THE LOCAL POLICE

Exam Review #3:   **7.** B   **8.** B

Part C: OBSERVATION AND REPORT WRITING

Exam Review #4:   **9.** C   **10.** **A.** (C) **B.** (C) **C.** (F) **D.** (F)

11. Who... What... Where... When.... How.... and Names of Witnesses

Part D: AUTHORITY TO QUESTION

Exam Review #5:   **12.** B   **13.** A   **14.** A

Part E:	INSPECTIONS

Exam Review #6: **15.** D   **16.** B   **17.** A

Part F:	LEGAL RESPONSIBILITIES (Liabilities)

Exam Review #7: **18.** A   **19.** B   **20.** B   **21.** A

Part G:	FACTORS TO CONSIDER BEFORE MAKING AN ARREST

Exam Review #8: **22.** D   **23.** D   **24.** B   **25.** A
26. B

Part H:	ARRESTABLE OFFENSES

Exam Review #9: **27.** A   **28.** A   **29.** B   **30.** A
31. A   **32.** B   **33.** A   **34.** B
35. A

Part I:	PRIVATE PERSON'S ARREST

Exam Review #10: **36.** B   **37.** A   **38.** B   **39.** A

Part J:	MAKING AN ARREST

Exam Review #11: **40.** D   **41.** A   **42.** A   **43.** D

Part K:	SEARCHING THE SUSPECT

Exam Review #12: **44.** A   **45.** B   **46.** A

Part L:	SEARCHING A SUSPECT UNDER THE MERCHANT'S PRIVILEGE RULE (No Exam Review Questions)

Part M:	AFTER THE ARREST

Exam Review #13: **47.** A   **48.** B   **49**. C   **50.** C
51. D

Part N: TERRORISM

Exam Review #14 **52.** A   **53.** A   **54.** D   **55.** D
                   56. A   **57.** B   **58.** A   **59.** A

Part O: ETHICS AND PROFESSIONAL CONDUCT

Exam Review #15 **60.** B   **61.** D   **62.** B   **63.** B
                   64. A

PART Q.

FINAL EXAMINATION

DIRECTIONS: Write your answers on the *ANSWER SHEET* provided.

DO NOT MARK ON THIS TEST

1. The security guard/proprietary private security officer's role *BEFORE* a violation has been committed is to:

   a. Watch and wait.
   b. Prevention.
   c. Apprehend and detain.
   d. Observe and report.

2. What is the security guard/proprietary private security officer's role *AFTER* a violation has been committed?

   a. Watch and wait.
   b. Search and seizure.
   c. Observe and report.
   d. Apprehend and detain.

3. Acting in such a way as to make someone think that you are a peace officer is:

   a. Illegal and should never be done.
   b. Permissible under special circumstances.
   c. Perfectly acceptable.
   d. Dangerous.

4. You are patrolling a company parking lot and see two people trespassing near a car on the lot. You should first:

    a. Arrest them for trespassing.
    b. Prevent them from leaving and call the police.
    c. Politely ask what they are doing.
    d. Ignore them.

5. Security officers have the same power to arrest as:

    a. Peace officers.
    b. Private persons (citizens).

6. Who can make a felony arrest?

    a. A peace officer.
    b. A security guard/proprietary private security officer.
    c. Other private persons.
    d. Any of the above.

7. If a security guard/proprietary private security officer uses too much force to make an arrest, he/she may be sued and/or have criminal charges filed against them.

    a. True
    b. False

8. When arresting a suspect for suspicion of burglary, you should say:

    a. "I am making an arrest."
    b. "You are under arrest for suspicion of burglary."
    c. Both a and b.

9. When you are not sure whether to detain or arrest, you should:

    a. Observe and report and not detain or arrest.
    b. Detain the suspect until the police get there.
    c. Search the suspect to find evidence to arrest him/her.
    d. Arrest the suspect for a misdemeanor.

10. If the suspect looks bigger and stronger, would that be a good reason for a security guard/proprietary private security officer not to make an arrest by himself/herself?

    a. Yes
    b. No

11. Can you search people before arresting them?

    a. Yes
    b. No

12. You are working as a security guard/proprietary private security officer at a factory. The owner thinks that some employees are stealing tools. The owner asks you to search their cars on the parking lot. Are you legally allowed to search their cars?

    a. Yes
    b. No

13. Are you allowed to reach in through an open car window to take out tools that may have been stolen?

    a. Yes
    b. No

14. When you make an arrest, you should call the police:

    a. After everyone has left the area.
    b. Without delay or as soon as possible.

15. As a security guard/proprietary private security officer, are your duties the same as a peace officer's?

    a. Yes
    b. No

16. In our legal system, innocence or guilt is decided only by a court.

    a. Yes
    b. No

17. Are you, or any private person, legally required to arrest a suspect once you have seen them commit a crime?

    a. Yes
    b. No

18. Can you search a person to try to find enough evidence to arrest him/her?

    a. Yes
    b. No

19. What police procedure is followed when a suspect is taken into custody?

    a. They take the suspect to the station and book him/her.
    b. They write a citation on the spot and then let the suspect go.
    c. They submit reports to the district attorney for handling.
    d. Any of the above depending on the offense.

20. If you make a legal citizen's arrest, are the police required by law to take custody of the suspect?

    a. Yes
    b. No

21. A *FELONY* crime is generally considered to be:

    a. A misdemeanor.
    b. A major crime.
    c. An infraction.
    d. A mistake.

22. A *MISDEMEANOR* crime is generally considered to be:

    a. A felony.
    b. A minor crime.
    c. An infraction.
    d. A mistake.

23. As a security guard/proprietary private security officer, you are meeting a primary responsibility when you:

    a. Observe safety hazards.
    b. Observe security violations.
    c. Report safety hazards and security violations.
    d. Do all of the above.

24. A security guard/proprietary private security officer's authority to question people on private property owned by his employer is:

    a. Greater than that of private parties.
    b. No more than any private person.
    c. The same as a peace officer.

25. The two conditions that must exist before a felony arrest can be made are: 1) that a felony crime must have been committed; and 2) you must have reason to believe the suspect actually committed the felony crime.

    a. Yes
    b. No

26. You witness a woman setting fire to a building. The offense she may have committed is:
    a. Arson.
    b. Burglary.
    c. Theft.
    d. Disturbing the peace.

27. A man in a bar is making obscene remarks and trying to start fights. The security guard/proprietary private security officer on duty asks the man to leave, but he refuses. The offense he may have committed is:

    a. Arson.
    b. Burglary.
    c. Theft.
    d. Disturbing the peace and trespassing.

28. A person breaks into a drug store late at night and takes several bottles of pills. What offense may have been committed?

    a. Arson.
    b. Burglary.
    c. Theft.
    d. Robbery.

29. An employee's husband waits in the parking lot by her car. When she arrives he hits her. What offense may have been committed?

    a. Battery.
    b. Verbal assault.
    c. Theft.
    d. Robbery.

30. Is a person with only a security guard registration allowed to carry a deadly weapon?

    a. Yes
    b. No

31. When searching a suspect, you may search for the following:

    a. Weapons only, when you have reasonable grounds to believe the suspect has a weapon.
    b. Contraband (narcotics).
    c. Personal property and identification.
    d. Anything that is in his or her pockets.

32. A woman tells you, "The suspect tried to kill the bus driver with a metal pipe." This statement is:

    a. A fact.
    b. A conclusion.

33. A person who has been arrested for robbery should be referred to as:

    a. The criminal.
    b. The suspect.
    c. The robber.
    d. All of the above.

34. You should not arrest a person for a misdemeanor unless that person has committed the offense in your presence.

    a. True
    b. False

35. Your wrongful acts as a security guard/proprietary private security officer may result in a liability lawsuit to include which of the following parties?

    a. You, the security guard/proprietary private security officer.
    b. Your employer.
    c. Other people involved.
    d. All of the above.

36. Terrorism is a use of force or violence against persons or property for the purpose of intimidation or coercion.

    a. True
    b. False

37. Are all acts of terrorism crimes?

    a. True
    b. False

38. What are the four counter terrorist techniques of physical security?

    a. Security, weapons, deadly force and threat intelligence.
    b. Deter, delay, deny and detect.
    c. Deadly force, minimum force, de-escalation of force and entry searches.
    d. None of the above.

39. What are the two types of terrorism?

    a. Chemical and Biological terrorism.
    b. Computer and Sabotage.
    c. Coercion and Fear.
    d. Domestic and International.

(Revised1 10/11)

40.   What are the characteristics of a terrorist?

    a. They will have a specific objective in mind.
    b. They will always conduct a surveillance of the target.
    c. They will rehearse their operation.
    d. All of the above.

41.   Appearance and cleanliness are not as important as showing up on time for work.
    a. True
    b. False

42.   The general public judges a security guard/proprietary private security officer by:

    a. Appearance.
    b. Speech.
    c. Attitude.
    d. All of the above.

43.   A security guard/proprietary private security officer's ability to fulfill their duties is dependent upon securing and maintaining public respect and approval.

    a. True
    b. False

44.   Accepting gratuity is acceptable at certain times.

    a. True
    b. False

STOP!
THIS IS THE END OF THE TEST

Please double-check your answers. Then turn your test and materials in to the person administering the exam.

POWER TO ARREST FINAL EXAMINATION
ANSWER SHEET

Date: _____

Applicant: _____   Instructor: _____

PLEASE MARK ALL OF YOUR ANSWERS WITH AN X.

1. A B C D	16. A B	31. A B C
2. A B C D	17. A B	32. A B
3. A B C D	18. A B	33. A B C D
4. A B C D	19. A B C D	34. A B
5. A B	20. A B	35. A B C D
6. A B C D	21. A B C D	36. A B
7. A B	22. A B C D	37. A B
8. A B C	23. A B C D	38. A B C D
9. A B C D	24. A B C	39. A B C D
10. A B	25. A B	40. A B C D
11. A B	26. A B C D	41. A B
12. A B	27. A B C D	42. A B C D
13. A B	28. A B C D	43. A B
14. A B	29. A B C D	44. A B
15. A B	30. A B	

POWER TO ARREST RECORD

This is to certify that the above applicant has been instructed in the Power to Arrest and that he has passed with a score of 100%. I understand that this answer sheet must be kept on file for two years and that the material will be reviewed during each audit performed by the Bureau of Security and Investigative Services. This also certifies that this applicant has been given a copy of "The Responsibilities of the Security guard/proprietary private security officer" as required by the Bureau of Security and Investigative Services.

_____   _____   _____
Instructor's Signature   Applicant's Signature   Applicant's Name (Printed)

(Revised1 10/11)

WEAPONS OF MASS DESTRUCTION

& Terrorism Awareness for Security Professionals

Student Workbook

State of
California
Department of
**Consumer
Affairs**

CALIFORNIA DEPARTMENT OF CONSUMER AFFAIRS

WEAPONS OF MASS DESTRUCTION AND TERRORISM AWARENESS FOR SECURITY PROFESSIONALS

Student Workbook
Version One

This publication and all related materials may not be reproduced, in whole or in part, in any form or by any means electronic or mechanical or by any information storage and retrieval system now known or hereafter invented, without prior written permission of the California Department of Consumer Affairs, Bureau of Security and Investigative Services (BSIS), with the following exception:

California licensed private or proprietary security agency or business providers, licensed and approved training facilities, and licensed instructors are allowed to copy this publication and related materials for non-commercial use in training professional security personnel pursuant to state law and regulation.

All other individuals, private businesses and corporations, public and private agencies and colleges, professional associations who are both in-state and out-of-state may obtain copies of this publication and related resource materials, at cost, from the Department of Consumer Affairs as listed below.

California Department of Consumer Affairs
Bureau of Security and Investigative Services
401 S Street, Suite 101
Sacramento, CA 95814

(916) 322-7530

or

www.dca.ca.gov

The U.S. Department of Homeland Security, Office for Domestic Preparedness (ODP), and the Governor's Office of Homeland Security (OHS) provided funds for the development of this course.

TABLE OF CONTENTS

This 4-hour training program is brought to you by the California Department of Consumer Affairs and the Governor's Office. As you are well aware, our country is threatened by potential terrorist activities. Potential targets are many, but they do have one thing in common: they are either locations of great economic importance or they are places where large numbers of people gather. In almost all cases, the places where you work could be either a target or a potential source of resources for terrorist criminals.

This training video, and its attendant activities, have been developed specifically for you. They are designed to make you more aware of what to look out for to help prevent future attacks. We invite you to participate fully in this important training and to ask questions of and provide suggestions to your facilitator.

You are essential for our security.

Before you participate in this training program, it is useful to preview what you think you might learn. Discuss the following questions in small groups.

1. What are some likely locations in California that could be targets of terrorist activity?

_____

_____

_____

_____

2. Why do you think those locations are likely targets?

_____

_____

_____

_____

3. How would you define terrorism?

_____

_____

_____

_____

4. What comes to mind when you hear the expression "Weapons of Mass Destruction?"

_____

_____

_____

_____

Part A.   Please answer the following 5 questions:

1. What is the purpose of terrorism?
    - ❏ a. to invade another country
    - ❏ b. to frighten a group of people
    - ❏ c. to propose a new religion

2. True or False: All terrorists have a religious purpose to their actions.
    - ❏ a. True
    - ❏ b. False

3. Why did the US customs agents become suspicious of Ahmed Ressam as he tried to cross the US/Canada border?
    - ❏ a. He acted hesitant and unsure.
    - ❏ b. He threatened them with a gun.
    - ❏ c. He was carrying explosives in his car.

4. Which of the following is <u>not</u> a purpose of a terrorist act?
    - ❏ a. to cause emotional pain in its victims
    - ❏ b. to cause economic damage
    - ❏ c. to test their weapons

5. Please check all the possible targets for a terrorist act from the list below:
    - ❏ a. government buildings
    - ❏ b. mass transit facilities
    - ❏ c. public buildings
    - ❏ d. communication facilities
    - ❏ e. utilities
    - ❏ f. water supply locations
    - ❏ g. food production sites
    - ❏ h. recreational facilities
    - ❏ i. a mall
    - ❏ j. a stadium
    - ❏ k. all of the above

Part B.   Small groups: Discuss the following

1.   Why would a terrorist target your workplace?

_____

_____

_____

_____

2.   What harm could come to California or the nation if a terrorist attack occurred at
     or near your workplace?

_____

_____

_____

_____

3.   When most people think of terrorism, they think of bombs. Can you think of any other
     means of frightening or harming large groups of people?

_____

_____

_____

_____

Part A.   Small group discussion.

1. Think of 3 ways in which a terrorist organization might try to recruit members at your workplace.

_____

_____

_____

2. Is there anything a terrorist could steal from your workplace that he could sell to make money?

_____

_____

_____

3. Under what circumstances would vehicles at your workplace, such as bicycles, cars, trucks, helicopters, or boats, make you suspicious?

_____

_____

_____

4. Think of ways in which a terrorist might be able to get onto your site without anyone noticing.

_____

_____

_____

Part B. True or False (and why)?

True False

❏ ❏ 1. Terrorist organizations do not recruit more members.

_____

_____

❏ ❏ 2. Terrorist organizations have all the money they will ever need.

_____

_____

❏ ❏ 3. A bomb is the most common terrorist weapon.

_____

_____

❏ ❏ 4. A terrorist attack is especially likely on a day of national significance.

_____

_____

❏ ❏ 5. A terrorist can gain access to a secure site by impersonating a uniformed professional.

_____

_____

❏ ❏ 6. Terrorists need to "case the joint" or conduct surveillance of their target.

_____

_____

❏ ❏ 7. To move a weapon into place, a terrorist always needs something large, like an airplane.

_____

_____

❏ ❏ 8. After an attack, the terrorists need to escape, unless it is a suicide attack.

_____

_____

"Devil's Advocate"

In this exercise, you will pretend to be an organization planning a mass attack using a Weapon of Mass Destruction on a chosen California site. Follow the steps below to plan your criminal event.

Scenario—You are a small but well-organized group of people who hate California and all it stands for. You could be a religious group, a political group, or any other special-interest group. You want Californians to fear and respect you and to accept you as their new leaders.

1. Begin your evil plan by looking for more members for your terrorist cell. How would you go about recruiting? (Think about some possible ways in which the site where you work as a security professional could be involved in the recruiting process.)

   _____

   _____

   _____

   _____

2. Start planning your budget. How will you get money? (Consider some ways in which the site where you work could have some relationship to the funding process.)

   _____

   _____

   _____

   _____

3. Choose your weapon(s). Describe them in detail. What are the components and where can you find them? (Think about some aspect of the weapon-creation process that might involve the site where you work.)

   _____

   _____

   _____

   _____

4. Select your target. You want to create maximum devastation and fear in the community. What would you select? (You may have to re-think your choice of weapon at this point if you decide that some other means, for example biological rather than explosive, would be more terrifying.)

_____

_____

_____

_____

5. Choose a date for your terrorist attack. Why did you choose that date?

_____

_____

_____

_____

6. Look at your target site. What information do you need to gather? How will you get onto the site unnoticed?

_____

_____

_____

_____

7. Now plan to move your selected weapon to the site you have identified. What means of transportation do you need? How many people? What kinds of identification or disguise?

_____

_____

_____

_____

8. Finally, you have been able to detonate the weapon. There is mass panic and devastation. How do you escape? (As a security officer, what do you think you would be doing at this point?)

_____

_____

_____

_____

The table below is the same you saw in the video training program. Some words have been replaced by a blank line. Fill in the blank lines with the 17 words and phrases listed here:

75%	Die	Low
Anthrax	Easy to make	Millions
Cheap	Explosives	Psychological
Chemical	Fire	Radiological
Chlorine	Group	Terrorists
Deploy	Impact	

WEAPON OF MASS DESTRUCTION	ADVANTAGES TO THE TERRORIST	DISADVANTAGES TO THE TERRORIST	EXAMPLES
Biological	• Cheap, _____ and easily available • Hard to detect in the victim population • Great _____ damage (fear)	• It takes a long time for effects to show up • It may hurt the _____ as well • People will get sick, but perhaps not many will ___ • They may not get much sympathy for their cause	• _____ • Botulism toxins • Cholera • Plague • Smallpox
Nuclear	• Devastating effects • Great psychological _____ • Escalates an attack to all-out war	• Heavy • Expensive (hundreds of _____ of dollars) • Very difficult to make and to deploy	• Death by nuclear explosion • Radiation burns • _____ poisoning • Long-term effects such as cancers
Incendiary	• Easy to make from home-made materials • Ignite about _____ of the time • Fire is very frightening	• Unless accompanied by the effect of a bombing, the victim population knows how to deal with _____ • The terrorist may destroy more property than lives	• Trigger methods can be _____, electronic, or mechanical • Delivery methods can be stationary, hand-thrown, or self-propelled
Chemical	• _____, easy to make and easily available • Has an immediate effect • Great psychological damage (fear)	• Need to have a lot to have a mass effect • Dangerous to produce and _____ for the terrorist	• Mustard • Cyanide • _____ • Sarin
Explosive	• Dramatic • _____ risk • Easy to execute remote attacks	• May damage both the intended _____ and innocent bystanders, such as babies • Not simple to make the attack covert	• Over 70% of domestic terrorist incidents involve _____ • Pipe bombs • Vehicle bombs • Suicide bombs

Discuss the scenario you just watched with your team members.

1. What was the reason for the traffic stop?

   _____

   _____

   _____

   _____

2. Which behaviors made the officer suspicious?

   _____

   _____

   _____

   _____

3. What did the officer find in the cab of the truck?

   _____

   _____

   _____

   _____

4. What did the officer find in the truck bed?

   _____

   _____

   _____

   _____

5. If you noticed people behaving like this at your site, what would you do?

   _____

   _____

   _____

   _____

1. Where should you find the contact information for whom to notify in an emergency? What is your back-up plan if you cannot reach the first person on your list?

   _____

   _____

   _____

   _____

2. At your site, who has the authority to order an evacuation?

   _____

   _____

   _____

   _____

3. If the person identified in question #2 is unavailable, what do you do?

   _____

   _____

   _____

   _____

4. What are secondary devices?

   _____

   _____

   _____

   _____

5. If you think airborne hazardous materials have been released, what path of evacuation would you take?

   _____

   _____

   _____

   _____

6. Why should you pay attention to people leaving the scene of the incident?

_____

_____

_____

_____

7. Which of the choices below is the concept of self-protective measures?

- ❏ 1. Time, distance, and wind direction
- ❏ 2. Time, distance and shielding
- ❏ 3. Speed, distance, and time
- ❏ 4. Protection, assistance, and speed

Please answer the following 10 questions by checking off the best answer and turn in the form to your training facilitator.

Name: _____

Date: _____

PROTECTING CALIFORNIA'S CRITICAL INFRASTRUCTURE

1. Which of the following sites in California are potential targets of a terrorist attack?

   ❏ a. Disneyland   ❏ c. Los Angeles International Airport

   ❏ b. The California aqueduct   ❏ d. All of the above

2. A terrorist attack is a

   ❏ a. threat   ❏ c. bomb

   ❏ b. crime   ❏ d. religious event

3. Which of the following examples is a biological agent?

   ❏ a. Anthrax   ❏ c. Sarin

   ❏ b. a radiological agent   ❏ d. a Molotov cocktail

4. Terrorists act on impulse.

   ❏ a. True   ❏ b. False

5. Which of the examples below is a chemical agent?

   ❏ a. Anthrax   ❏ c. Chlorine

   ❏ b. Uranium   ❏ d. Dynamite

6. What percentage of terrorist incidents involve explosives?

   ❏ a. None   ❏ c. 50%

   ❏ b. 5%   ❏ d. Over 70%

7. Should you be suspicious of someone showing interest in when you make your rounds and what you do?

    ❏ a. No   ❏ b.Yes

8. In the case of an apparent chemical incident, what should you <u>not</u> do?

    ❏ a. Report the incident to your supervisor   ❏ c. Determine the wind direction

    ❏ b. Inform the police   ❏ d. Rush in to try to help the victims

9. What information is critical for you to perform your job in an emergency?

    ❏ a. Knowing your shift time   ❏ c. Knowing your supervisor's name

    ❏ b. Knowing your post orders   ❏ d. Knowing the name of the terrorist group

10. Which three words describe your role in protecting your site as a security professional?

    ❏ a. Recognize, report, react   ❏ c. Hot, warm, cold

    ❏ b. Time, distance, shielding   ❏ d. Explosive, nuclear, biological

THANK YOU. PLEASE TURN IN THIS FORM TO YOUR FACILITATOR.

acquire to obtain, to get

acute intense, sudden

aftermath the time after an event

agent in this context: a substance or a cause

Al Queda the name of a terrorist organization

anthrax a bacterial biological agent

arson illegal use of fire

bacteria single-celled organisms that can cause illness in people, plants, and animals

biological agents a bacteria, virus, or toxin used as a weapon

blasting caps the part of an explosive device that sets off the detonation

B-NICE Biological, Nuclear, Incendiary, Chemical, Explosive

botulism toxins a nerve poison that causes serious paralytic illness

CBRNE Chemical, Biological, Radioactive, Nuclear, Explosive

chemical agents a chemical substance used as a weapon

chlorine a commonly-used disinfectant, highly toxic as an inhalation hazard

cholera an illness cause by a bacterial infection

common denominators characteristics that events or objects have in common

contaminated poisoned

covert hidden or secret

credentials in this context: identification documents

cryptic not easily understood, obscure

cyanide a highly toxic chemical

detonation blast, explosion

devastation destruction

disrupt to disturb

dry run a practice event

escalate to increase

evacuate to send people away to safety

excerpt a piece or segment of something

explosive a bomb

first responder emergency personnel and trained security professionals

hazardous dangerous

ID theft stealing someone's identification

ignite to start to burn

ill-gotten gains something that has been stolen

impersonate to pretend to be someone else

incendiary devices things that start a fire

infectious disease-causing agent a substance that causes a disease that spreads easily

isolate to keep someone away from others

landline a telephone connected through a cable; not a cellular phone

liaison a connection

mass transit group vehicles, such as buses, trains, planes

mustard agent phosgene gas used in World War I

nuclear weapons an atomic bomb

plague an infectious disease caused by bacteria

pre-incident indicators events that suggest that something is about to happen

radiological material substances that can cause illness or death which come from an atom with an unstable nucleus decaying until it becomes stable and releasing radiation

rally a public meeting

retaliation revenge

sarin a synthetic chemical warfare agent classified as a nerve agent

scenario a situation

secondary devices something that is intended to explode after the initial attack to cause further damage

self-propelled moving by itself, such as for example a rocket

shielding protection

shrapnel pieces of metal blasting out from an explosive device

smallpox a contagious and sometimes fatal disease cause by a virus

stationary standing still

suicide killing oneself

supremacist someone who thinks he is by nature better that other types of people, for example people of other races

surveillance observing an area or a situation

symbolic figurative, representative

symptom an indication or a sign

symptomatic indicative

to push an objective to strongly propose something

toxic poisonous

toxin a poisonous substance

trigger methods methods of exploding something

utility facilities buildings and infrastructure for electricity, water, gas, etc.

viable possible, working

vigilant observant

virus an illness-causing organism smaller than a bacteria

vulnerabilities defenselessness, exposure, weakness

California Department of Consumer Affairs

TERRORISM QUICK REFERENCE CARD

Security officers should be aware of suspicious factors that may indicate a possible terrorist threat. These factors should be considered collectively in assessing a possible threat. This quick reference guide is intended to provide practical information for you but may not encompass every threat or circumstance. Follow your post orders to contact someone for assistance or information.

SUSPICIOUS FACTORS TO CONSIDER

1. **Possible Suicide Bomber Indicators—A.L.E.R.T.**

   A. **A**lone and nervous

   B. **L**oose and/or bulky clothing (may not fit weather conditions)

   C. **E**xposed wires (possibly through sleeve)

   D. **R**igid mid-section (explosive device or may be carrying a rifle)

   E. **T**ightened hands (may hold detonation device)

2. **Passport History**

   A. Recent travel overseas to countries that sponsor terrorism

   B. Multiple passports with different countries/names (caution: suspect may have dual citizenship)

   C. Altered passport numbers or photo substitutions; pages have been removed

3. **Other Identification—Suspicious Characteristics**

   A. No current or fixed address; fraudulent/altered: Social Security cards, visas, licenses, etc; multiple IDs with names spelled differently

   B. International drivers' ID

   1. There are no international or UN drivers' licenses— they are called permits

   2. Official international drivers' permits are valid for one year from entry into the U.S., they are paper-gray in color, not laminated, and are only valid for foreign nationals to operate in the U.S.

4. **Employment/School/Training**

   A. No obvious signs of employment

   B. Possess student visa but not English proficient

   C. An indication of military type training in weapons or self-defense

Fold here

5. **Unusual Items in Vehicles/Residences**

   A. Training manuals; flight, scuba, explosive, military, or extremist literature

   B. Blueprints (subject may have no affiliation with architecture)

   C. Photographs/diagrams of specific high profile targets or infrastructures; to include entrances/exits of buildings, bridges, power/water plants, routes, security cameras, subway/sewer, and underground systems

   D. Photos/pictures of known terrorists

   E. Numerous prepaid calling cards and/or cell phones

   F. Global Positioning Satellite (GPS) unit

   G. Multiple hotel receipts

   H. Financial records indicating overseas wire transfers

   I. Rental vehicles (cash transactions on receipts; living locally but renting)

6. **Potential Props**

   A. Baby stroller or shopping cart

   B. Suspicious bag/backpack, golf bag

   C. Bulky vest or belt

7. **Hotel/motel visits**

   A. Unusual requests, such as:
   1. Refusal of maid service
   2. Asking for a specific view of bridges, airports, military/government installation (for observation purposes)
   3. Electronic surveillance equipment in room

   B. Suspicious or unusual items left behind

   C. Use of lobby or other pay phone instead of room phone

8. **Recruitment techniques**

   CAUTION: the following factors, which may constitute activity protected by the United States Constitution, should only be considered in the context of other suspicious activity and not be the sole basis for security officer action.

   A. Public demonstrations and rallies

   B. Information about new groups forming

   C. Posters, fliers, and underground publications

9. **Thefts, Purchases, or Discovery of:**

   A. Weapons/explosive materials

   B. Camera/surveillance equipment

   C. Vehicles (to include rentals—fraudulent name; or failure to return vehicle)

   D. Radios: short-wave, two-way and scanners

   E. Identity documents (State IDs, passports, etc.)

   F. Unauthorized uniforms

Cut on dotted line

Cut on dotted line

BUREAU OF SECURITY AND INVESTIGATIVE SERVICES
P.O. Box 980550
West Sacramento, CA 95798-0550
(916) 322-4000
www.bsis.ca.gov

REPORT OF INCIDENT
(Private Investigator, Private Patrol Operator, Security Guard, Alarm Company, &
Alarm Agent)

Any incident involving a physical altercation or the use of a deadly weapon while on duty by licensees, qualified managers, officers, partners, or employees must be reported to the Bureau of Security and Investigative Services within seven (7) days of the incident, pursuant to Business and Professions Code sections 7521.5(b), 7583.2 (g), 7583.4, and 7599.42. The information provided will be used to investigate the incident to determine if further Bureau action is necessary. If a violation of law is established, disciplinary action may be initiated as provided by the Business and Professions Code.

A deadly weapon is defined to include any instrument or weapon commonly known as a blackjack, slingshot, billy club, sandclub, sandbag, metal knuckles, any dirk or dagger, any firearm, any knife having a blade longer than five inches, any razor with an unguarded blade and any metal pipe or bar used or intended to be used as a club.

PERSON INVOLVED IN PHYSICAL ALTERCATION OR USING DEADLY WEAPON

NAME: Last First Middle	DATE OF BIRTH: (month/day/year)
ADDRESS: Number and Street City	State Zip
TELEPHONE NO. (optional): Home Cell	E-MAIL ADDRESS (if applicable):
REGISTRATION/LICENSE NO.:	EXPIRATION DATE:
DEADLY WEAPON PERMIT NO.: (IF REQUIRED):	EXPIRATION DATE:
CALIBER(S) ON PERMIT (IF FIREARM):	TYPE OF DEADLY WEAPON OR CALIBER OF FIREARM USED:

LICENSEE (COMPANY) INFORMATION

COMPANY NAME:	LICENSE NO.:
ADDRESS: Number and Street City	State Zip
CONTACT PERSON:	TITLE:
TELEPHONE NO.:	

INSURANCE INFORMATION
This section must be completed if there was a firearm involved in any incident involving a private patrol operator licensee or security guard. A private investigator must complete this section if there was a firearm incident while performing bodyguard duties.

Liability insurance is required of private patrol licensees who employ armed personnel, pursuant to Business and Professions Code sections 7583.39, 7583.40, 7583.42. "Insurance policy" means a contract of liability insurance issued by an insurance company authorized to transact business in this state, and which provides minimum limits of insurance of $500,000 for any one loss due to bodily injury or death and $500,000 for any one loss due to injury or destruction of property.

NAME OF INSURANCE COMPANY:	POLICY NUMBER:
ADDRESS: Number and Street City	State Zip
POLICY EFFECTIVE DATE:	TELEPHONE NUMBER:

(SEE OTHER SIDE)

INCIDENT INFORMATION

Complete all information. Use a separate sheet of paper, if necessary.

1. Date of incident: _____   Time: _____

2. Where did the incident occur? _____

    Business name or post location: _____

                        NUMBER AND STREET   CITY   STATE   ZIP
    Address: _____

    Telephone: _____   Type of Business: _____

3. Was a police or sheriff report taken?   Yes _____   No _____

    If yes, name of agency: _____

    Report Number: _____   Officer's Name: _____

4. Was there a citation or arrest?   Yes _____   No _____

    If yes, what charge(s) and against whom? _____

    _____

5. **DETAILS OF INCIDENT:** Include circumstances leading to physical altercation or use or discharge of firearm, injuries, deaths, name of suspect, number of shots fired, names and addresses of witnesses, and discipline imposed by employer. You must clearly describe any injuries and damages. You must also identify all participants. Use a separate sheet of paper, if necessary.

_____

_____

_____

_____

_____

_____

_____

_____

_____

READ THE FOLLOWING CAREFULLY BEFORE SIGNING. I hereby declare under penalty of perjury, under the laws of the State of California, that the statements in this report are true and correct. I understand that all statements herein are subject to investigation.

Print Name: _____

Signature: _____   Date: _____

Employer Signature: _____   Date: _____

    Title: _____

Back